GARDENING WITH
T·R·E·E·S

SONIA KINAHAN

CHRISTOPHER HELM
London

© 1990 Sonia Kinahan
Line illustrations by Shona Grant
Christopher Helm (Publishers) Ltd, Imperial House,
21–25 North Street, Bromley, Kent BR1 1SD

ISBN 0–7470–1801–4

A CIP catalogue record for this book
is available from the British Library

Typeset by Opus, Oxford.
Printed and bound in Great Britain by Butler & Tanner, Frome, Somerset

CONTENTS

Figures

Colour Plates

Acknowledgements

My thanks to the following for their help and advice during the writing of this book: Hastings Public Library; Seaford Public Library; Jim Keesing, Living Collections Division, Kew Gardens; Dr Brent Elliott, Librarian of the Royal Horticultural Society's Lindley Library; Mr Baker, Wisley Fruit Officer, Wisley; Mrs Dealtrey, British Association of Rose Breeders; Mr Graham Rice; my sister, Pamela Campbell.

Sonia Kinahan
Heathersett
Norfolk

*To my dear daughters, Deirdre, Vanessa and Melanie —
my three 'trees' for the future*

Illustrations nos. 2, 3, 5, 6, 9, 10, 12, 16, 19, 20, 23, 25, 27, and 28 are reproduced courtesy of John Glover.

An Introduction on How to Use This Book

In all the magnificent great gardens and parks, the large trees play the most important role, the focal point of the whole setting for both the house and the landscape. And this effect is still vital to aim for, whatever size of garden you may be blessed with; great thought should go into the choosing and selection of site of this essential element of your own garden design.

I suppose the oak is the first tree everyone thinks of in England — perhaps nothing can equal a full-grown oak of great age, especially in an English setting; and every country has its favourite, in warmer climates the noble cypress graces the landscape. But the setting any of these great trees make in this landscape can still give ideas as to what to plan for in a garden area of much smaller dimensions.

To grow a tree and see it getting taller, and thicker in the trunk, every year, is one of the most satisfying experiences that a gardener can have. I remember the first time I walked around the only garden I have owned myself and my hand moved over the smooth silkiness of the silver beech bark, and the crustiness of the apple bough. I really felt then that it meant something to possess a garden and that I had a duty now to look after these trees and see they were not damaged or cut down unnecessarily. And this I have tried to do, feeling I must put their welfare before mine and not follow those who have sold off pieces of their gardens to make their lives financially easier — where the trees are often cut down, sacrificed to put a building in the place they had grown in, and which they had graced for so many years. Of course, people need somewhere to live, but so do trees; and they can't speak for themselves and many take longer to mature than we do.

When it was suggested to me that I write a book on trees, I realised that the subject is so vast that the only way to tackle it was to choose as many of the trees that I could find that I would like to grow myself or had already grown in the garden. Then, when thinking and finding out more about those trees that initially take the fancy, the reader would be led on, as when looking up a word in a dictionary or an encyclopaedia, to track down something I have not

1

mentioned that seems particularly attractive. In this way you will make up your own list of favourite trees and then you can plan how, in the garden you have, or hope to have one day, you will plant these specimens and see them either grow to maturity and frame the picture you had in your mind when you started; or that you know will one day reach their potential for others who come after you to enjoy and perhaps recall 'I remember who planted that lovely tree'.

Though the idea of growing a tree sounds a little daunting, there are so many sorts of trees that can be planted to mature quickly and give balance, form and decoration to the modern domestic garden, however small. Nowadays, new varieties have been selected for growing where there is little space; these will soon attain a reasonable size and yet, with judicious pruning, will not dwarf the garden, or their roots take over and damage the surrounding plants and buildings. Maturity time can be cut down if a plant is purchased several years old, and with a pot-grown specimen planting can be done at any time of the year, as long as care is given to watering. An interesting new discovery is that trees grow better when they are not heavily staked; a slight rocking from the wind encourages the tree to put down stronger roots faster, so giving a better root-stock. If some staking is necessary in a very windy situation, a short stake placed at an angle so as not to pierce the root will hold the bottom of the trunk firm and leave the top of the tree to move about, and then it seems to grow well. This is a complete reversal of the old-time practice, as is the idea of not painting cut branches with a wood paint, but leaving the tree to produce its own protective seal.

By carefully choosing the kind of tree you want for the space you have, and placing it for best effect among surrounding shrubs and plants, you can create your own plant picture. So everyone can grow and enjoy the possession of a few trees in their own garden, without waiting too many years to see the result. Evidence of this is particularly striking in Japan, where the smallest plot will be made into a tiny garden with a tree gracing the design.

You will see I have not included conifers, except the Ginkgo. To describe them all would have needed another book to itself, and as this is a very personal choice — and I must admit I am not so fond of conifers — I have found the range of other trees to describe more than enough.

When I mention a Zone, the number I give is the lowest one they will grow in with ease, but of course with careful siting and protection, you can get a tree to thrive in certainly one lower Zone number.

In the main chapter the trees are listed alphabetically for easy reference, but I have not done this in the short chapter on fruit, so as to make it less formal.

Finally, you will not find chemicals of any kind mentioned in this book. I do not believe in using any, but try by careful management and the use of natural preventatives, to ensure that the trees will live in harmony with the environment, and conserve our land, unpolluted, for future generations to enjoy.

CHAPTER 1
Selected Trees in Alphabetical Order

ACACIA

I think my favourite tree for its bright scented flowers is the acacia, but unfortunately, it needs continuous sunshine and lack of frost to grow to its full size. There are nearly 1,000 species throughout the world, the majority of them native to Australia; but they are seen in abundance all around the Mediterranean region, and in California and Florida in North America.

But they can be grown successfully in favoured sites of the British Isles and I have known of large 30 ft (10 m) trees in North Wales and in various parts of the south of England, including my own county of Sussex. This variety is *A. dealbata*, or Silver Wattle, the name the plants are known by in Australia. The evergreen feathery pale green leaves give a very delicate effect all year, and in February, in the northern hemisphere, the sprays of bright fluffy yellow balls of flowers give off a most fragrant and heady perfume.

Personally, I have found this mimosa a difficult one to grow out of doors even with the benefit of sea air, as the cold winter winds — which are more severe in the south-east than in the south-west of England — seem to frizzle the fine tender leaves and the plant loses them as well as the flower-buds in a cold winter. But, if the early part of the winter has been wet and warm and therefore the sap is soft in the stem, I bind the stem for 2 ft (60 cm) above the ground which stops the bark splitting — with no protection, should a heavy frost ensue, the bark splits and rarely recovers. The same thing happened with my tree ceanothus because I failed to wrap up the main trunk. However, my felt-protected *A. dealbata* has survived, bark unsplit, and I shall tie the branches close to the house wall for added shelter as they grow, hoping for a mild winter when the tree will reward me, and the flowers blossom. I know it can be done for not a mile away a similar but older tree, as high as the house it is planted against, blooms every year, tucked into a corner of two walls for added warmth. Perhaps it has the best of both worlds, the benefit of mild coastal air, but away from sea wind damage.

My favourite variety was, I thought, *A. longifolia* which has similar flowers but long slim leaves. I was uncertain of its name as I was given a plant by a friend, from a large tree he grew locally and which set seed. It became too large for its pot in the greenhouse and I planted it near the front gate, only protected for 3 ft (1 m) of the lower part by an oak fence. It grew to at least 12 ft (4 m) and flowered almost continuously the year round for several years. It died after the hot dry summer of 1976 which was very strange as these trees are used to great drought in their native land. Undaunted, I got another, identical plant, which I brought home from a hillside in Provence where 6 in (15 cm) high seedlings were growing wild *en masse*. I gave it the pride of place in the garden, facing full south in a cosy corner where two walls meet. It grew very fast and was flowering heavily, loaded with flower and leaf, when one autumn night a southerly gale brought it down by hitting the walls and bouncing off behind and against the poor mimosa and snapping the tall stem 4 ft (1.2 m) from the base. To my great regret it has not broken leaf again, but I keep the stump as a souvenir, and it makes a very useful stake and base for a *Clematis balearica* which has formed a triangular dome over it, graced the year round with evergreen bronzy leaves, and sweet apple-green flowers all winter. But I shall try a mimosa again, for a garden must be an exciting, challenging place and if only 'playing-safe' trees are planted you may lose interest in them and there is nothing to watch out for — a sudden and unexpected flowering; a bashing from the wind when your tree will need help by temporary staking and perhaps the construction of a little wigwam of hessian, to enable a small plant to get on its feet again; or a sudden collapse, or curling of leaves, when thought must be given as to remedies — more watering of the roots, feeding and foliar feeding or looking for insect damage, or sometimes even animal damage.

So, although I was given the first of these two trees as *A. longifolia*, I now believe they were *A. rhetinodes*, as the former has long spires of flowers and my plants had round balls like the common *A. dealbata* which *A. rhetinodes* does have. And it is the most lime-tolerant of the mimosas and I have heavy clay soil, so perhaps that is why it grew so fast, only to be beaten by severe patches of weather. But I had months of pleasure from these trees, with their bright yellow scented flowers, before their demise. Now I have been given some seeds of *A. baileyana*, the Cootamundra Wattle, with very attractive glaucous leaves and deep yellow racemes of flower through winter and spring. These seeds need to be split by placing in boiling water to soften the hard casing. Similarly, if you cut sprays of mimosa for the house, the stems should be dipped in boiling water for a moment to help delay the desiccation of the fluffy balls.

ACER

The acer or maple is composed of a genus of over 200 species, with a prolific number of varieties. They are very hardy — the majority easy as to soil — and are grown mainly for their brilliant leaf colours in autumn, since on the whole their flowers are unobtrusive. They range from tiny cascading plants no more than 12 in (30 cm) high to the great trees of the forest areas; so there is a maple for every plantation and garden whatever the size. The leaves are wide and in opposite pairs off the stem, some with lobes varying from three to seven in different species.

I will describe a few of the acers I have seen and admired, but the choice is so wide that it is best to decide for yourself the one that takes your fancy, perhaps growing in a beautiful garden, or a nursery; for the variation in leaf and colour and type of bark, apart from the size, is so dramatic that only a personal choice will satisfy the discerning gardener.

Acer means 'sharp' in Latin and the trees are so-called because their wood once made good spears for fighting. The seed cases — known as keys or samaras — are all slightly different in each species.

Acer negundo, the Box Elder or Ash-leaved Maple from Northern America and Canada, is very tough, tolerating Zone 2 and grows very quickly to become a well-shaped tree, but is short-lived. The leaves, unlike other maples, are pinnate, composed of three or five leaflets and are a fresh green. At one time its sugar was used a great deal to provide maple syrup. The green flowers come before the leaves, the females in drooping clusters, the males upright, on separate trees. The winged fruit called 'spinning jennies' remain on the bare branches after the leaves have fallen, turning a pale coffee colour. The variety *A. negundo* 'Auratum' has vivid chrome-yellow leaves which hold their colour well all through the summer; and one I particularly admire is *A. negundo violaceum* which can have as many as seven leaflets, the young growths violet, touched with a white frosty look. In spring a mass of deep pink blooms hang from the branches of this lovely tree.

A. griseum, from the mountains of Central China and Zone 5, is known as the Paperbark Maple because the old dark brown bark flakes and reveals a delightful orangey-copper smooth new bark beneath. The twigs are unusually wiry and slim; the leaves, composed of three leaflets 2–3 in (5.8 cm) long, dark green and very hairy, in autumn become one of the most stunning of all the maples, turning a brilliant scarlet and orange and really lighting up the garden. The fruits are unusually large, the wings being 1½ in (4 cm) long.

A. palmatum (with bright green leaves like palms), the Japanese Maple and originally from China, Japan and Korea, has many varieties. But the leaves are not all the same shape or colour. I saw a beautiful small tree of *A. palmatum* 'Dissectum Atropurpureum', with its dark purple cut foliage, cascading over a large rockery, and making a real feature. This species prefers a more acid soil, and a sheltered site to protect the delicate sprays of leaves.

A. rubrum, the Red Maple or Canadian Maple from eastern North America, and able to withstand Zone 3, requires an acid soil to do well because on chalk it does not produce such a good bright red leaf-colour in autumn, these being first dark green with a bluish tinge beneath, 3- or 5-lobed and up to 5 in (12 cm) long. When it does colour well, it gives such a fine contrast to the grey bark. It is a quick grower, 80–100 ft (25–30 m) or more in the ideal surroundings of its own habitat but very much smaller in cultivation, and is elegantly dressed in spring with its scarlet blooms, the fruits being of the same colour when they come. Though the flowers are small, their massed clusters make a stunning overall cloud of crimson.

But there are two desirable varieties that are ideal for the garden, *A. rubrum*

'Schlesingeri' gives wonderful bright red autumn colour and makes a nicely shaped tree. And when planted near evergreens, gives lovely contrast of colour. If space is very limited, plant *A. rubrum* 'Scanlon', it is a real treasure, growing straight up to form a narrow column of foliage, again a brilliant red in autumn.

Another good maple for the smaller garden is *A. pensylvanicum*, the Striped or Snake-bark Maple or Moosewood, from the same area and tolerating the same Zone 3 as *A. rubrum* but nowhere near so tall, 20–40 ft (6–12 m). It does not grow well in a chalky soil, but has a striking bark of white stripes against the green of the trunk — which is, unbelievably, the bright colour of jade — just as soon as the branches are a couple of years old. The rich green leaves are 3-lobed and large, as long as 7 in (18 cm) and about 6 in (15 cm) wide, and become a rich gold in autumn.

If you want a quick-growing tree it takes a lot to beat the Sycamore, *A. pseudoplatanus*, seen growing everywhere in the British Isles, Europe and Western Asia and tolerating Zone 5, and it will reach 20–30 ft (6–10 m) very rapidly. (Incidentally, in Scotland it is called the Plane.) Though a native of Europe it was only introduced into the British Isles by the Romans. The 5–7-lobed leaves are toothed and bronze at first, then dark green, with the hanging blooms a greenish-yellow. The variety *A. pseudoplatanus* 'Brilliantissimum' is small and much slower-growing and also has lovely colours of leaf. They become green in autumn, having first appeared with a pinky tinge, and during the summer changing to a soft greeny-yellow. This elegant tree does better in a site that is a little shaded. Similarly, *A. pseudoplatanus* 'Worleei', the Golden Sycamore, has greeny-yellow spring leaves, turning golden and finally a pure green before falling. The beautifully smooth and creamy wood of this species is used in many ways from the making of fine musical instruments to furniture.

A. ginnala, from China and the Amur River district and Zone 2, is a very desirable small tree, for it has sweetly scented creamy flowers during May. The leaves are 3-lobed, quite small and dark green with red ribs, and as the tree forks low on the trunk the effect is of a large bush. But the autumn colour of the leaves is richly flame-coloured, as are the showy keys.

Acers propagate well by seed, too effectively sometimes, as their winged seeds are spread everywhere by the wind; but their varieties must be grafted.

AESCULUS

One of the finest sights in late spring, in parks and large gardens and bordering the avenues, is the beautiful flowering Horse Chestnut or Buckeye tree. But my pleasure is tempered by an experience I had in a house I lived in once with a small walled garden. Three chestnut trees, probably growing from its dropped fruits or 'conkers', had taken root just the other side of one wall and completely blocked out light and sun, and made the garden dripping and damp. We could not get these trees trimmed or lopped by our neighbour and so the garden was a 'write-off' as nothing would grow and even in summer it was chill and damp. So they are not trees to be planted indiscriminately in the average garden; but fortunately there are varieties with more modest growth that will do well instead. The most common variety, *A. hippocastanum*, attaining when fully mature around 100 ft (30 m), has huge white candle-like inflorescences standing well clear of the foliage; these leaves are palmate, usually 5 or 7 leaflets, toothed and radiating from the stalk-end, and there is a double form *A. hippocastanum* 'Baumannii', which does not have conkers, which may or may not be a blessing. But a much smaller-growing variety 'Pumila' would be the best one to plant in limited space.

A. glaucescens has greeny-yellow flowers, the underneath of the leaves covered with a fine bloom, and this grows only slowly, 6–10 ft (2–3 m) tall.

My favourite has red flowers and this Red Buckeye, *A. pavia*, blooms in June, the variety 'Atrosanguinea' having flowers of an even darker red and the whole tree not exceeding 10 ft (3 m). A cross between the two species has produced a very desirable deep pink-flowered but compact tree, though eventually growing to 20 ft (6 m), *A. × carnea* 'Briotii'. *A. parviflora* is smaller-growing, almost shrub-like in form and making a dome of foliage and flowering in July and August with scented white flowers, dramatized even more clearly by red anthers.

There are many more species of these trees to choose from, with varying shades of flower and leaf, several colouring well before they fall. They are found in most parts of the world from the Zone 7 of California to areas of Zone 3; but what we think of as a common tree in England is actually native to the area between northern Greece and Albania, though very hardy to Zone 3. Similarly, *A. pavia*, although native to the south-eastern parts of the United States, can be grown much further north to Zone 5. But perhaps one of the loveliest and smallest-growing is *A. neglecta georgina*, from this same part of the States, with reddish-orange blooms and only attaining 4–6 ft (1.2–2 m) when mature.

AILANTHUS

The Tree of Heaven, *Ailanthus altissima*, its name meaning 'the tree that can grow up to the sky', is one of a genus of eight, and a very impressive specimen with its huge leaves, pinnate in form. It is usually seen in parks and is very easy as to type of soil and grows happily in the centre of cities, in sun or partial shade, reaching 60–70 ft (18–20 m) in height. Though it is a fast grower, its rate of growth does slow down in later years and, if kept hard-pruned each spring, in a garden border it will make a small tree bearing even larger elegant leaves which can reach 3 ft (1 m) in length. The flowers are greenish-white and not very conspicuous, but it is best to plant the female form, for this will produce bunches of bright red fruits. When allowed free-rein it gives a dramatic effect on a lawn, the smooth grey bark indented with clefts. But in the average garden it must be carefully sited and controlled, with suckers and seedlings rigorously removed, or you will regret planting it. The variety *A. altissima* 'Pendulifolia' makes a beautiful weeping tree with its enormous fronds of hanging leaves.

There are glands under each individual leaflet and if squeezed the oil within gives off an unpleasant smell, as do the flowers.

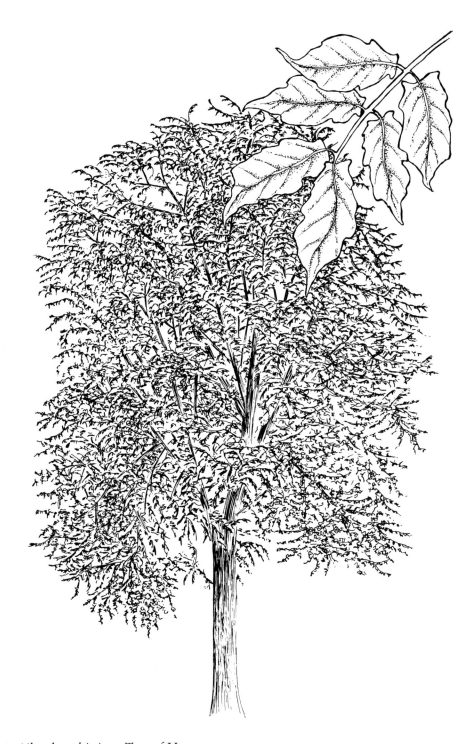

1 *Ailanthus altissima*: Tree of Heaven

ALBIZIA

The albizia, with the lovely name of the Persian Silk Tree, is a relation of the mimosas and at first glance can be mistaken for *Acacia dealbata*, for the feathery sprays of leaves are very similar. There are many species, mostly grown in the tropics, but *A. julibrissin*, found from Iran to China, is remarkably hardy, tolerating some frost, but it needs a hot sunny summer to produce the curious pink flowers, like a powder-puff at the end of a branch, for several weeks from June onwards. Later come fruit in the form of long seed pods. The variety *A. julibrissin* 'Rosea', from Korea, has a deeper rose colour to the stamens and is more compact in growth, not developing so widely across as the paler one and so useful in a confined space, and easier to protect should the weather require it. It is hardier, anyway, to Zone 5, but it grows best in the South of England against a warm wall, and really needs the Mediterranean area to be seen in its full glory. Given ideal conditions, I think it is a very pretty tree indeed, and with its wide-spreading form of growth graces and gives shade to the streets of southern cities.

ALNUS

The alders are often seen growing near the water's edge of streams and ponds, for the majority of them like deep moist soil. *A. cordata*, the Italian Alder, will tolerate a drier situation in the British Isles, for it is a native of Corsica and southern Italy and grows rapidly to 30 ft (10 m) or more in a very elegant tapering shape. The leaves are dark and glossy and heart-shaped. Male and female catkins appear on the same tree, the male appearing in March before the leaves, in clusters of three and nearly 3 in (8 cm) long. The fruits come eventually in erect groups like cones, and producing the largest ones of all the alder species.

The common European alder, *A. glutinosa*, so-named because of the stickiness of the leaves when young, is often seen along river banks, with its yellow catkins in March. There is a pretty form with yellow leaves in spring, *A. glutinosa* 'Aurea', and particularly attractive is *A. glutinosa* 'Imperialis' with totally different, delicate feathery leaves, giving a much more ethereal touch and would not have such a 'heavy' feel in an average-sized garden.

The American Speckled Alder or Grey Alder, *A. incana*, is an even hardier species, tolerating Zone 2 and found also in Europe and the Caucasus. It has a polished grey bark, whereas the common alder's is of an uneven texture and much darker. The leaves, too, are never sticky, but with a grey down beneath. A colourful variety and a choice one to plant is *A. incana* 'Aurea', a neater-growing form than the *A. glutinosa* 'Aurea' and keeping the yellow colour overall but touched with red on the catkins which appear in February. But if you want a weeping tree which will form a solid mass down to the ground of greenish-yellow foliage, and not grow too large, *A. incana* 'Pendula' will produce its catkins as early as January. Then the Himalayan Alder *A. nitida* makes a magnificent tree up to 100 ft (30 m) with huge shiny ovate leaves as long as 6 in (15 cm), but, unusually and usefully, flowering in September.

2 *Albizia julibrissin*: Persian Silk Tree

Because it tolerates wet conditions so well when growing, the wood of alder trees is very durable and so is often used for underwater constructions such as breakwaters and landing stages. For this reason, too, it was used years ago for the manufacture of the shoes known as clogs, and its charcoal is incorporated into fireworks.

AMELANCHIER

The amelanchier is one of the nicest trees for the smaller garden. Also known as the June Berry or Snowy Mespilus, of roughly a dozen species — some of which are shrub in form — most prefer lime-free soils, but four will tolerate a certain amount of lime if the ground is well-drained and kept moist, though not dry chalk soil. Of these, perhaps *A. asiatica*, the Chinese June Berry, is the choicest as it flowers over a longer period, and then there are blackcurrant-like fruits. But the one that makes the best tree, especially if the side shoots only are pruned, to encourage a taller growth, is *A. lamarckii* which produces white flowers along the branches in May before the first leaves appear, copper in colour, turning to green during the summer, then yellow and bright scarlet before they fall. The flowers produce red berries which turn black and are edible. So this is a very showy small tree on which there is something to watch out for all summer. The white flowers give it its 'snowy' name, but there is an attractive pink-flowered form, *A. lamarckii* 'Rubescens', a richer pink when in bud. If you can provide a sheltered site it does help to protect the cascades of flowers from cold winds, but otherwise it is hardy to Zone 4.

In North America the amelanchiers are known as Shadblows because it is said they flower at the same time as the shad fish comes up river to spawn in April.

ARALIA

There are about 20 deciduous species in the genus *Aralia*, some of them shrubby in form, but all with enormous spectacular dark green leaves on long thorny branches. *A. elata*, known as the Japanese Angelica Tree, makes a handsome tree if the suckers are removed so that a nice main stem can form and then the 3 ft (1 m) long compound leaves, composed of ovate leaflets about 4 in (10 cm) long, which are crowded at the end of the branches, drape gracefully downwards. In late summer tiny white flowers, in 1–2 ft (30–60 cm) long panicles, top the branches. Later come fruits that look like tiny blackberries. There are two variegated-leaf forms, one with yellow markings and the other cream, but both gradually bleach to an indifferent shiny white and I do not find them very attractive, as I am not partial to varigated leaves in any plant.

A. chinensis, the Chinese Angelica Tree, is similar, and in some books is referred to as the same tree, but the flowers appear a little earlier in umbellate racemes. The trunks of the aralia can be spiny, and there is a variety, *A. spinosa*, Hercules' Club or Devil's Walking Stick, which hails from the south-eastern part of the United States. Unfortunately, this tree has particularly spiny stems, but it flowers even earlier, in June or July, so that it has produced its fruit by the time

3 *Amelanchier lamarckii*: Snowy Mespilus

the Chinese and Japanese trees come into flower. The white blooms are tinged with green, but are not so decorative.

These trees are quick growers, though not usually reaching more than 20 ft (6 m) in Great Britain, but twice this height in their native conditions. They should not be planted in too rich a soil or they will become sappy and not stand the winter so well; though hardy, tolerating Zones 3 and 4, they must be protected from chilly winds to avoid damage to the leaves. Place in sun or partial shade and, because of the size of the sprays of leaves, the best position would be somewhere where the full effect of leaf and flower can be viewed from a reasonable distance. They all do well in city conditions. The thorny suckers should be pulled up as soon as possible and can be used for propagation. Any pruning should be carried out in the spring, to keep the tree in shape and to the size you want it for the position and space you have chosen for it.

ARBUTUS

Some years ago, after a particularly wild storm of westerly gales, I thought I had lost my treasured Strawberry Tree, the *Arbutus unedo*. One enormous limb was torn off by the wind and for ages it looked very lop-sided but gradually the re-growth began and soon it was completly restored to a solid mass of evergreen, some 15 ft (5 m) tall and across, a good backcloth to the surrounding shrubs and other plants all the year round. In October it is covered with bunches of waxy-white flowers like lily of the valley and, if the birds haven't stripped them completely, the fruits from last year's blooms are also on the tree. These are yellow at first, turning orange and then red as they ripen. So amongst white flowers there are also these three different colours gradually ripening among the matt dark green serrated leaves. These fruits are edible and are made into a kind of jam in Corsica. *A. unedo* 'Rubra' is a form with very attractive pink flowers.

There are several varieties apart from *A. unedo*, which is also known as the Killarney Strawberry Tree where it grows wild on the islands and shores of the lakes there, being happy in any mild coastal district. Inland, it is sometimes killed to the ground in severe winters, but breaks again from the root. I have seen trees lining the roadsides in a riot of colour along the coast of Provence in the South of France. The Greek form, *A. andrachne*, though tender as a young plant, becomes hardier if it is given a decent position with some protection against cold winds. And the fascinating red-brown of its bark is present in a very desirable hybrid between the last two forms, known as *A. × andrach-noides*. So choose your site carefully for whatever variety you decide to grow, for the arbutus does not like to be moved once established and initially is best planted from a pot.

A very much taller-growing tree and one that flowers in the spring is *A. menziesii*, the Madrona of California. It is the tallest not only of the arbutus trees, but of all the heath family. It has been known to grow to around 100 ft (30 m) high in the wild. But the fruits are only half the size of *A. unedo*, and it is not happy in a limy soil, whereas the other varieties, despite coming from the ericaceous family, are remarkably tolerant. My tree is growing in heavy clay, but fortunately in a very well-drained position at the top of a sloping lawn.

BETULA

The birch is a genus of about 40 deciduous trees and shrubs which grow in varying zones, from the Temperate of 7 to the Arctic as harsh as 2. They are the hardiest broad-leaf tree, and the only species native to Greenland and Iceland, and do better on deep non-chalky soil, but otherwise are very easy to cultivate.

Birches are renowned for their attractive barks and rich yellow autumn leaves. They produce male and female catkins on the same tree, the males being formed in the autumn, expanding in spring to the well-known 'lamb tails'. They are an ideal tree for a moderate-sized garden, growing quickly to 30–50 ft (10–15 m) as long as they have good light, for they do not like to be in the shade of other trees. The most often planted is the Silver Birch, *B. pendula*, or the European White Birch, also called the Lady of the Woods and tolerant of Zone 2. With its elegant tracery of drooping branches and toothed triangular-shaped leaves above a silvery-white trunk which peels attractively, it makes an ideal specimen for a lawn, either on its own, or if you have the space, a small group is very effective. The twigs are hairless, unlike other birches, with resinous warts. The flowers open in March, male catkins 1¼ in (3 cm) long, the female ½–1 in (1.2–2.5 cm). The latter ripen to 1–1¼ in (2.5–3 cm) long and hang from the trees very attractively until they break up in the autumn and winter, shedding winged 3-lobed bracts. One of its most desirable varieties is Young's Weeping Birch, *B. pendula* 'Youngii', where the growth is very compact and dome-like and the branches are even more pendulous, sweeping the ground.

The birches are not deeply rooted, so do not thrive well on very dry shallow soils, *B. pendula* being the most tolerant of such conditions; in fact one species, *B. nigra*, the Red Birch or River Birch from eastern United States and Zone 4, likes a damp site, though not too wet of course. This tree does not have a white or silvery bark but one that is creamy and cinnamon-coloured at first, gradually becoming nearly black, very rough and coarse. This peels in winter revealing a smooth pinky-brown young bark underneath. It grows tall and often pyramid-shaped, but sometimes produces many stems from ground level. The leaves are the characteristic saw-edged diamond shape, but slimmer, light green and shiny on top, with a down on the underside veins. The flowers come about a month later than *B. pendula*, the male catkins 2–3 in (5–8 cm) long, the females only ½ in (1.2 cm), but as they ripen they extend to 1–1½ in (2.5–4 cm), become downy and are held erect on short stems. These ripen as early as June, so that the seeds fall and germinate at a time when river waters are likely to be low; for their favourite site is along river banks.

Another birch, with an absolutely pure-white bark going right up into the smallest branches at the head of the tree, is *B. papyrifera*, the Paper Birch or Canoe Birch, from North America and Zone 2, so-called because its shiny aromatic bark strips off like sheets of paper revealing a pale orange below. And the Red Indians used the waterproof bark for making canoes. The dark green leaves are hairy, with black glandular dots on the undersides, turning a more striking yellow in autumn than *B. pendula*. And the male catkins can be 4 in (10 cm) long. It makes a large tree, but there is a variety *B. papyrifera minor* which only grows to form a short bushy tree, and this would make an elegant planting where space is limited.

B. utilis, the Himalayan Birch, comes from the eastern Himalayas and China, and has either a dark brown or creamy-copper bark and, although said to be only tolerant of Zone 7, a tree has survived in the Edinburgh Botanic Garden in Scotland. But give it protection from late spring frosts if possible when young, by planting on a slope. This tree is worth trying on chalk. From the western Himalayas comes *B. jacquemontii* with one of the most striking white barks of all, which peels off in transverse strips. Its leaves are ovate, doubly toothed and smooth, whereas *B. utilis* are dark green above with a hairy underside.

B. nana, the Dwarf Birch, is a charming little native tree only 2 ft (60 cm) tall with small circular dark green leaves and erect catkins in April; ideal in a tiny garden. And a recent introduction shown at the Chelsea Flower Show in London in May 1988 is a charming small birch, *B. alba* 'Golden Cloud', which gives a really bright splash of gold to the garden scene.

B. pendula, being a native, is a good tree to grow in Britain as it is not so susceptible to insects, which will infest *B. utilis*, for example, because it comes from abroad and has not built up any defence against the native pests.

Propagate by seed in February pushed into the top surface of the soil.

Be careful when you plant your birch if you have a small garden, because it will deprive nearby plants of any goodness you may have added to the soil. Site the tree on the verges of your ground, or on a banked edge, and then it will only add decoration and grace to the general scene.

BUDDLEIA

A most effective way of producing a focal point in a garden, which I saw and much admired when visiting someone several years ago, was the design of a raised bed some 3 ft (1 m) high, made into a kidney shape and centred around a tree of *Buddleia alternifolia*, the Fountain Buddleia. Most of the buddleias, because they are hard-pruned each year, are thought of as shrubs, but this *B. alternifolia* had been trained, by selecting a good stem, into a lovely weeping standard. The sweet-smelling lilac flowers, with their heliotrope scent which attracts butterflies, moths and bees, hung over the beds below, the tree having been planted in the crook of the kidney-shaped bed, which was faced on all sides with rocks and over which draped low-growing plants. The general effect was a dramatic eye-catcher in this garden and made me realise how important it is to place the few trees you may have room for in really dominant and striking positions. There is a variety of *B. alternifolia* named 'Argentea' with a very attractive sheen on the leaves from silk-like hairs.

B. globosa, the Chilean Orange Ball Tree, makes an upright little tree as it must not be pruned in spring unlike the *B. davidii* shrub group, for it sets flowers on the old wood of the previous year. I had quite an old specimen tree, some 15 ft (5 m) high, which produced masses of bright orange honey-scented distinctive balls of flower, and made quite a feature of that part of the garden in June. Unfortunately, a helpful relative pruned it really hard and it gave up the struggle, for it was of some age and had a very gnarled stem, and it did not break from the trunk again as I hoped it would.

A third buddleia that will make a small decorative tree is *B. colvilei*, from the Himalayas. If you can get it through its youth it becomes reasonably hardy and able to withstand quite severe winters. Then in June bell-shaped rose-red flowers appear at the end of the branch tips. It likes a really sunny position and does particularly well on a gravelly soil. If you prefer darker richer red flowers the form *B. colvilei* 'Kewensis' was developed some years ago.

CARPINUS

The name carpinus is said to derive from the use of the wood at one time to make oxen yokes, *carr* being the Celtic for wood and *pen* meaning head. It is commonly known as the Hornbeam and consists of a genus of over 20 species, all deciduous, and related to the filberts, and which grow happily in any soil, even heavy wet ones, and can be planted in full sun or partial shade.

C. betulus is native to most of Europe and Asia Minor and is also found in many areas of Southern England, particularly Epping Forest. It is tolerant of Zone 5 and has a very hard fine-grained wood, used in a variety of ways, including for the striking hammers in pianos. It makes a handsome specimen planted on its own, but is often used for hedging and pleaching, and will retain its new growth of leaves throughout the winter — like the beech hedge — if cut

4 *Buddleia alternifolia*: Fountain Buddleia

with shears at the beginning of August. When grown as a free-standing tree, *C. betulus* first develops a pyramid shape, gradually broadening out. It has a grey trunk like the beech, but not quite so smooth, and vertically grooved with brown on older trees. Two other differences are the fruits that are hop-like in appearance — and turn brown in November; and the doubly toothed leaves, 2–3 in (5–8 cm) long, oval with a pointed tip. These colour a soft yellow in autumn, being first rich dark green with conspicuously ribbed veins. The flowers open in March, the females from the tips of growing shoots, the males elegant catkins 1½ in (4 cm) long, which have been enclosed all winter inside buds.

This tree grows rather too large for the average garden, but some of its varieties are more suitable in height and girth. *C. betulus* 'Columnaris' has a shape said to be remindful of the Lombardy poplar, is slow-growing and very neat and close in form. Not quite so small a tree and also not so slow-growing is *C. betulus* 'Fastigiata' but it rarely reaches 25–30 ft (8–10 m) after two decades. It is like *C. betulus* 'Columnaris' when a young tree, but becomes a little wider, but also a very beautiful shape. As the 3-lobed papery bracts — each containing a tiny ridged nut — remain on the tree after the leaf fall, this is another very obvious sign that it is a hornbeam and not a beech, for even though they can look similar in many ways they are not of the same family.

The Japanese Hornbeam, *C. japonica*, tolerating a little hardier Zone 4, is a very attractive species, never growing too large but with a nice expansive shape. The leaves are up to 4 in (10 cm) long, much darker and narrower than the European tree and have very prominent veins, and there are dramatic long-lasting fruiting catkins of 2–2½ in (5–6 cm) long inward-curving bracts, with a colour change from green, then tinged with pink and finally a rich red in autumn. The lovely smooth bark is a greyish-pink, or it can be dark with lighter grooving. This tree is best planted in some shade and then the leaves turn and remain a richer yellow colour.

The American Hornbeam, Blue Beech, Ironwood or Water Beech, *C. caroliniana* from eastern North America, is a good one to grow if you want a tough little tree tolerating Zone 2, with the fluted grey bark, and wide-spreading branches which dip down at the ends. The fresh green tapered leaves turn flame before falling, and the fruiting catkins can be as long as 5 in (12 cm).

Propagate hornbeams by seed in spring sown under glass, or they can be layered or radical suckers used; but the varieties need to be grafted.

CASTANEA

Castanea consists of about 12 species but the one seen often in the British Isles is *C. sativa*, the Sweet Chestnut or Spanish Chestnut, thought to have been brought here from Italy by the Romans. This tree grows comparatively quickly — 35 ft (10.5 m) in around 20 years — and anyway is exceptionally long-lived so it should be planted well away from a building, for it develops a thick trunk beautifully grooved in a right-handed spiral when allowed to grow to maturity. But it is often used for coppicing and indeed makes an effective and protective screen in a garden. The long serrated shiny leaves, with well-marked side-veins,

5 *Castanea sativa* 'Albomarginata': Sweet Chestnut

become crowded with sprays of yellowish-green catkins of flower in July. Unfortunately, it does not often produce a good crop of the edible nuts except in the countries bordering the Mediterranean, the summers of England generally being not quite warm enough. In fact the best variety for chestnuts is *C. sativa* 'Marron de Lyon', bearing nuts when a young tree and used for the mouth-watering sweetmeat *marrons glacés* so famous in France. There are two varieties, one with cream and one with yellow edges to the leaves. This tree, despite needing warmer climes to fruit well, is reasonably hardy to Zone 5 and will grow easily, even in a dry soil; it is fairly tolerant of lime but not happy on chalk. The nuts are enclosed in a jacket covered with spines, unlike the horse-chestnut — which anyway is not of the same family — and which has smooth jackets covering the nuts.

In the United States, *C. sativa* is susceptible to blight and the Chinese chestnut *C. mollissima*, or the Japanese form *C. crenata*, should be planted. But the best one to grow is the hybrid *C. mollissima* × *neglecta*, as the nuts are larger and a better flavour.

At one time we nearly bought a house with a sweet chestnut tree in the garden, and it looked so attractive gracing the lawn. But it had reached such a size that it dominated the area — in fact made a feature of it. There was also a preservation order on this tree which, laudable as this was, we felt that its proximity to the nearby wall of the house and the shade below its branches meant it had outgrown its position and might become a problem, not a joy to see as it should be. Perhaps the roots had begun to affect the foundations of the house, and not many flowering plants would grow below the shade of its beautiful leaves. So it is always necessary to think of the future when planting trees in a garden. Check and remember the size they may obtain in years to come, and whether they have the kind of roots that may disrupt nearby walls or foundations of buildings.

CATALPA

One of my first recollections, before I knew anything about gardening or took the interest my father was always urging me to, was the sight of the beautiful *Catalpa bignonioides*, the Indian Bean Tree, with its enormous leaves clothing the branches, and the wide, as well as tall shape, gracing a lawn in the grounds of a large house where the lawn sloped down to the river Thames at Henley near Oxford. Though it looks tropical with its great leaves, this tree is remarkably tough and a native of Asia and North America. Because the leaves are so large it is wise to make sure the tree is not exposed to blistering winds which will tear them to shreds. But cold it will tolerate, up to Zone 4.

Fortunately the catalpa grows fairly rapidly, for it does not flower well until it has reached 8–10 ft (2.5–3 m) high. Then in July and August the blooms come at the end of shoots in large clusters of white, spotted with purple and yellow. They are very like the flowers of the paulownia tree, fox-glove-shaped, except that they hang down in bunches, whereas the paulownia flowers remain erect. The huge leaves are heart-shaped, the undersides downy. The new growth is tinged with purple and a nice foil against the fresh green of the mature

6 *Catalpa bignonioides* 'Aurea': Golden Indian Bean Tree

growth. The variety *C. bignonioides* 'Aurea' has yellow leaves and is a magnificent sight with its soft golden pubescent foliage in a mature specimen, though this is slower-growing.

C. speciosa, the Western Catalpa, has larger flowers, though there are fewer of them in the bunch; but it flowers earlier and is hardier. The growth is more erect and twice the height of *C. bignonioides*. If the space you have is very limited you could grow a very attractive form of the latter, *C. bignonioides* 'Nana', which can be grafted as a standard and grown to produce a neat round dome, giving a really eye-catching focus to a small area. And there are several other species and hybrids of this delightful tree. The slim long beany pods, filled with white-haired seeds, follow the flowers and remain on the tree all winter. Altogether a stunning and unusually effective tree to grow and one which provides a real 'talking point' when walking around the garden.

CEANOTHUS

The genus of ceanothus are commonly known as the Californian Lilacs. The majority of them are shrubby in form, either prostrate or making lovely wall plants, where they appreciate the shelter given; against a greenhouse or a small building they will go up and over a roof, making a fine sight. But there is one true variety that develops into a magnificent evergreen tree, *C. arboreus*, which, in the right conditions grows quickly reaching 20 ft (6 m) high or more with a

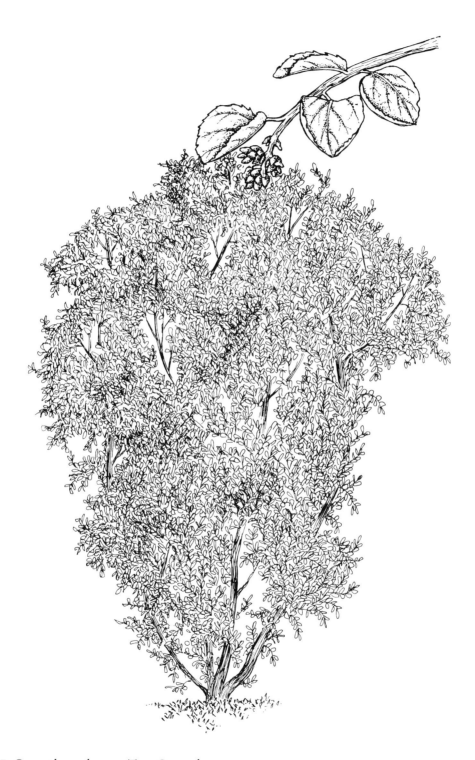

7 *Ceanothus arboreus*: Tree Ceanothus

thick trunk and large, oval, serrated and thickly veined glossy leaves, downy underneath. The flowers are bright blue, the size of lilac blooms, and in the variety which originated from the gardens it is named after in Cornwall in south-west England, *C. arboreus* 'Trewithen Blue', the flowers are slightly scented, the deep blue panicles fading slightly as they age; and it is slightly hardier.

In the southern counties of England these trees will survive if given sufficient shelter in full sun, and will do well near the coast. What they cannot tolerate is cold wet heavy soil, but they do not like shallow chalk either. The ideal is a light dry soil well-drained, even poor and stony, and a certain amount of lime can be tolerated. The best time to plant is in the spring, so that they have the summer to establish before facing the winter. They flower in spring mainly but I have found they produce blooms at any time of the year. My tree reached over 12 ft (4 m) before being blasted by an exceptionally cold winter, but I had planted it in a free-standing position down the slope of a lawn, partly sheltered from the north but it needed more protection than that to see it through a period of biting winds. On the same latitude, not 60 miles (90 km) away, I know of another 'Trewithen Blue' which has been sensibly planted in the corner where two 4 ft (1.2 m) walls meet and this tree has been the talk of the town for some time, a mass of blue flowers most of the year, with a 10 in (25 cm) trunk and the height and spread of the branches at least 25 ft (8 m) square. From a distance it is a cloud of blue, the leaves thickly crowding the branches, too. I shall plant my next attempt against the southern wall of my house and this will give it the best chance. The only snag is that when a southerly gale hits the wall, as it did with my mimosa tree, it bounces back behind the plant or tree growing there and tries to force it forward on to the ground. I ought to have leaned about this from experience long ago, for I had two *Escallonia macrantha* bushes, which had grown to tree size, and survived many years either side of the front entrance of the house. They always flowered profusely and provided shelter for surrounding plants, only to be pole-axed one night in a fierce storm.

C. arboreus can be allowed to grow freely, lower branches being taken off to make a good trunk and any pruning done in the spring after the main flowering. The large tree mentioned above grew so abundantly that whole limbs had to be lopped off to enable the owners to get through the garden gate!

CEDRELA

Cedrela sinensis, the Chinese Toon or Chinese Cedar, which is a near neighbour botanically of the attractive Tree of Heaven *Ailanthus altissima*, has the inestimable benefit of delightfully scented flowers, and leaves with a modest and not offensive onion perfume. Look out for it gracefully lining the boulevards of Paris, as it is also tolerant of industrial atmospheres. Its immense 1 ft (30 cm) long hanging bunches of individually small flowers are rather like those of the *Koelreuteria paniculata*, but with a delicate perfume. The plant has a lovely yellow hue, particularly in autumn, and a handsome specimen of this tree can be seen at Kew Gardens in London.

Though it is not quite so hardy as the ailanthus, it grows fairly quickly,

8 *Cedrela sinensis*: Chinese Cedar

becoming a nicely rounded tree; a pleasure to see in any garden. With its finely cut leaves it is also closely allied to the black walnut.

CERCIDIPHYLLUM

This is a pretty deciduous tree, native to Japan and China, the name being derived from the genus *Cercis* and the Greek word *phyllon*, meaning leaf, because the rounded leaves resemble those of some species of *Cercis*, but they are opposite and smaller. It is not, however, related to the *Cercis*, being more nearly allied to the magnolia than any other group.

C. *japonicum*, known as the Katsura Tree, will grow to 100 ft (30 m) in the wild, being the largest deciduous tree in Japan. It is found also all over Europe and in New England, USA, where it is mostly grown for ornament reaching about 50 ft (15 m), though in Japan it yields a valuable, light, soft fine-grained timber.

In Britain it only grows to a small or medium size with slightly pendulous branches when young, which become almost horizontal when mature, giving a nice pyramidal outline. The male and female flowers are on separate trees, and open in April before the leaves unfold. The males have groups of 15–20 red stamens and the females 3–5 twisted red styles, which grow longer during the summer and form fruit pods.

But the main feature of this tree is the lovely leaf colour. The young foliage is pinky-red, turning green during summer and in October producing gorgeous shades of amber, red, orange and purple. At the same time it emits a deliciously pungent sweet scent which gives it its common name of the Toffee-Apple Tree.

There is a form from China C. *sinense* which is much larger and has a single trunk unlike C. *japonicum* which is sometimes many stemmed. C. *magnificum* from Japan is very rare but has a lovely smooth bark and larger, more heart-shaped leaves with coarser serrations, and lovely yellow autumn colour. But C. *japonicum* is by far the hardiest and the best one to try in Britain.

This tree needs a sheltered site as it is sensitive to late spring frosts and should be planted in moist well-drained neutral soil, if possible slightly on the acid side. But it will tolerate Zone 4 and can withstand drought and likes to be in sun or semi-shade.

Propogate by seed in February, or by layering and softwood cuttings in summer. No pruning is needed beyond a little for shaping, at any time of the year, when necessary.

CERCIS

I am always fascinated by the extraordinary sight of my Judas Tree, *Cercis siliquastrum*, for the flower buds erupt from the bare stems of the branches and in May there is a cloud of purple covering the tree. A most effective sight against the blue sky. In a well-drained sunny position, my tree has reached 20 ft (6 m) and tolerates quite severe conditions in winter. As the flowers finish, the fresh green heart-shaped leaves come, and then there are red pods. The cercis is a very old tree from southern Europe and there is a good white form C. *siliquastrum*

9 *Cercidiphyllum japonicum*: Katsura Tree

'Alba' with paler green leaves, and *C. siliquastrum* 'Bodnant' with very deep purple flowers.

There are about six other species, the North American Redbud having richer green leaves but pale pink flowers; though it does need cold winters and hot summers to ripen the wood, so it is not such a successful flowerer in England.

CHIONANTHUS

The Fringe Tree is a delightful tree from a small genus of only two deciduous species, one from China and the other native to the other side of the world in North America, and found from Pennsylvania to Florida and Texas.

C. retusus, the Chinese Fringe Tree, grows to around 30 ft (10 m) in its native habitat, but 15–20 ft (5–6 m) in cultivation in Britain. It makes a handsome spreading tree which produces a mass of snowy-white flowers in June and July. These are five slim petals joined at the base, rather like those of the Witch Hazel, which gives a delicate spidery effect, but in such profusion it looks like snow. The fruits which follow in September are ovate and bluey-purple with one seed inside. They are not unlike an olive, and chionanthus does in fact belong to the olive family. The leaves are slim and oval and pointed, about 4 in (10 cm) long, and appear quite late on the tree, followed almost immediately by the flowers.

C. virginicus is slightly hardier and from Zone 4, and known as the North American Fringe Tree and also Old Man's Beard, because the blooms hang down to a point, looser and coarser than the Chinese species, but slightly fragrant and appearing a little earlier than *G. retusus*. The leaves are larger, narrower and oblong, a rich green above, paler and hairy beneath. The fruit is also slightly larger, nearly 1 in (2.5 cm) long, whereas the Chinese one is about ½ in (1.2 cm).

Both these trees need a rich deep neutral soil and a sunny position and then they are quite hardy and easy to grow, making 8–10 ft (2.5–3 m) in about 20 years. They are not very common, but I think they should be planted more often for their 'snow' of pure-white blooms looks quite stunning in the summer sun; one snag though, you do not get flowers — which have sexes on separate trees — on very young plants.

Propagation is from seed sown in February with *C. virginicus*, and by grafting upon the root of *C. retusus* in May. No regular pruning is necessary, but thin out crowded wood to ensure shapely plants.

CORNUS

The cornus, dogwood or cornel consists of about 40 species, many famous for their brightly coloured barks; though not all are trees, some like *C. canadensis* consisting of 6 in (15 cm) high shrubby ground-cover. A tree I like very much, as it flowers during winter, is *C. mas*, the Cornelian Cherry. On a bleak February day it can light up the surrounding garden, its delicate branches clothed with sulphur-yellow blooms. It makes a very effective specimen in the centre of a lawn trained to a single trunk; but left to itself it develops several and

1 *Acacia dealbata*: Mimosa

2 *Aesculus hippocastanum*: Horse Chestnut

3 *Aesculus x carnea*: Red Horse Chestnut

4 *Amelanchier lamarckii*: Snowy Mespilus

5 *Aralia elata* 'Variegata': Japanese Angelica Tree

10 *Chionanthus virginicus*: North American Fringe Tree

can form a useful thickety shrub. The leaves turn a rich colour before falling and in a good hot summer it will produce fruits like rose-hips which can be, and are, used for cooking in Southern Europe.

C. *kousa*, the Japanese Dogwood, grows into a small tree and from afar I once mistook this for a magnolia in flower; the creamy-white pointed bracts surrounding the insignificant flowers appear like luminous stars and as the tree I saw was planted at the bottom of a series of steps, I approached it from above, and so was able to see it to the best advantage as it flowered in June. There is a variety with a more upright, looser growth and larger inflorescences and leaves, C. *kousa chinensis*, which is even more attractive. The leaves of both become a crimson-bronze at the end of the summer, and the fruits resemble strawberries, but do not have their lovely flavour.

C. *nuttallii*, flowering in May, has numerous large bracts which turn pink with age. Though a giant of the Oregon and Californian forest trees reaching 75 ft (23 m) in North America, it does not grow very much beyond 15 ft (5 m) in the British Isles. So it is ideally suitable for a medium-sized garden when planted in a well-drained but moist soil of a good mix; a sheltered site would protect the fragile bracts from wind-damage. These leaves can sometimes turn red, also, late in the season, but more often a nice nut-yellow. All these three are easy as to type of soil, only C. *kousa* preferring a more acid mixture.

There are several other species with slightly different colourings and style of growth, C. *florida alba* and C. *florida rubra* with white or red bracts being particularly noteworthy. But one that attracts me is an evergreen and rather tender cornus, C. *capitata* from China and India and known as Bentham's Cornel. The oblong dull leathery leaves are downy underneath, and the tiny greenish flowers are surrounded by four large pale yellow bracts. The 1 in (2.5 cm) fruit that follow give this tree another show of colour in October and beyond, for they often remain on the tree through the winter, resembling something between a raspberry and a strawberry. Choose a warm frost-protected place in the garden for this tree unless you live in a favoured area, and then you will be able to keep it evergreen and stop the leaves reddening and dropping. But if this should happen do not despair, for it will recover in the spring and perhaps the next winter will be less fierce and worth waiting for. I find that, unless we take some chances in the garden, as with other things, we will not have the rewards.

CORYLUS

The corylus or hazel is a genus of about 15 deciduous species, most of which produce sweet edible nuts which are very nutritious, and these bushy trees are, also, very attractive to have in the garden.

C. *avellana*, the Hazel or Cob, is native to Europe and Asia minor and very hardy to Zone 3. It grows easily in any rich well-drained soil, in sun or shade, is very wind-tolerant, and can reach 20 ft (6 m) with a grey-brown trunk. But it is often seen in shrub-like form with more than one stem, for it can be hard-pruned to make a screen or hedge, and the pliant branches are used to

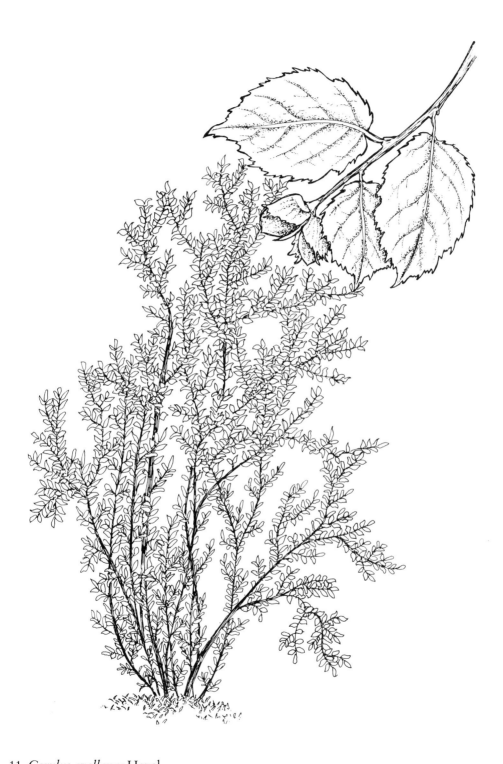

11 *Corylus avellana*: Hazel

make hurdles. It is grown prolifically in England, and particularly in the county of Kent for the commercial production of nuts. The trees need to be six years old before they bear their nuts, but then go on cropping for 50 years or more. In addition to its fruit it has decorative leaves which are almost circular, heavily veined and toothed, a hairy soft sage-green, turning yellow in autumn. The female flowers are tiny buds which in early spring produce small crimson tassels — in fact, the stigmas which protrude from the ends. The males, appearing on the same tree, small and fat in autumn, become lovely yellow hanging catkins 2–2½ in (5–6 cm) long, which in February shed their pollen. By October the round nuts have ripened, usually in groups of 2–4, the pointed ends just visible from inside their frilly-edged jackets. These trees are best grown on the edge of a garden, as a useful screen, for they can spread and be too untidy for a formal area.

But a slow-growing variety reaching only 10 ft (3 m) and planted for its extraordinary appearance is *C. avellana* 'Contorta', the Corkscrew Hazel or Sir Harry Lauder's Walking Stick. Not only does it have stunning bright lemon-yellow catkins in winter, but surrounding these are the slim branches, writhing and twisting into the most curious shapes like an indoor firework snake. So this needs siting near the house in order that the effect can be seen and enjoyed in winter.

The Filbert, *C. maxima*, from south-eastern Europe and western Asia, is more robust than the hazel and grows a little taller with larger heart-shaped leaves and longer nuts, oviod and oblong, and easily distinguished from the cob by the enveloping husk which completely covers the nut, extending beyond the apex. In fact, these species have often been cross-bred, so that the nut known as the Kentish Cob is really a filbert (Lambert's Filbert).

A very choice variety is *C. maxima* 'Purpurea', the Purple-leaf Filbert or Purple Hazel. The leaves are large and broad, a better colour than the 'Copper Beech' and can be 5 in (12 cm) long. They have an attractive down on them when young and the catkins come in February or March, depending on the weather and the position in the garden the tree enjoys. These catkins are a rich crimson, 4 in (10 cm) long and this tree makes an excellent planting for the border, for though it can reach 15–20 ft (5–6 m), if it is cut down annually this encourages it to produce desirably large leaves; and if the lower leaves turn green they should be removed, so that the overall purple colour is maintained. It normally takes seven years before it produces good nuts.

A corylus that makes a really handsome tree, triangular in growth, is *C. colurna*, the Turkish Hazel or Constantinople Nut, with greyish-brown scaling bark. The leaves are dark green and pointed with downy hairs on the underveins, and twice the size, being 4–5 in (10–12 cm) long and more deeply indented. It likes hot summers and cold winters, tolerating Zone 4; then the 3 in (8 cm) yellowy-brown catkins make a fine display during the bleakest of days, and it produces a good crop of nuts, grouped in threes or more, with their distinctive bristly and fringed husk. This tree is by far the largest and most ornamental of all the hazels, and can grow to 70–80 ft (20–25 m) in full sun.

A little more tender, only tolerating Zone 5, is *C. californica* the Californian Hazel, and although not reaching more than 10 ft (3 m) it is such an elegant species to have with beautifully soft velvety leaves. The bristly nuts are like the Turkish Hazel but with a protruding snout.

To propagate hazels, they can be tip-layered; or rooted suckers removed in autumn; or these trees will grow well from seed. And how satisfactory it is to have nuts in the garden, which have so many culinary uses.

COTONEASTER

Cotoneasters are very colourful plants, both evergreen and deciduous, and mostly shrub-like in form. But one or two grow to tree-size and can be trained to a single trunk by removing the lower branches to encourage this. Cotoneaster is related to the crataegus and the pyracantha, but does not have the nasty spines on the stems. From pink buds most of the white flowers appear in June and it is a particularly choice plant for those gardeners who wish to attract bees and butterflies to their garden; for on a hot sunny day the bees mass on the corymbs of flower, and as you pass under or near the tree you can hear the buzz as they work away.

The deciduous *C. frigidus* makes a nicely shaped dome above a single trained stem with oblong elliptical matt leaves. In September, crimson berries crowd the tree and often remain all winter, being so numerous even the feeding birds cannot spoil their bright display. There are some very choice hybrids of the Watereri Group which are semi-evergreen, that is they only lose their leaves in a harsh winter, and are hardy in Zone 7. C. × 'John Waterer' makes a small tree no more than 15 ft (5 m) but spreading to around 10 ft (3 m), the branches crowded with red berries. Another with the fattest red berries of all is C. × 'Cornubia'; C. × 'Inchmery' has yellow berries which take on a pinkish tinge with time; but perhaps the most versatile cotoneaster to grow, when trained on a stem, is C. 'Hybridus Pendulus' a lovely sight of red and green when the bright red fruits cover the trailing branches of glossy green leaves. It will also do well in a tub and is ideal for a corner of a small town garden, especially those that have some shade to contend with. Cotoneasters are not fussy with their requirements so are useful to bear in mind for a difficult corner of any garden. They really prefer sun, though they will grow in partial shade, and any soil will suit them.

CRATAEGUS

This is a large species of some hundreds of deciduous shrubs and a few trees, none of these growing more than 20–30 ft (6–10 m) and some are very small, but still genuine trees. The Common Hawthorn, Quick or May of the hedgerows, *C. monogyna*, can be useful in a garden as a barrier, for its vicious thorns deter any unwanted visitor. In May the crataegus is covered in a mass of headily scented bisexual flowers like tiny roses — it does, in fact, belong to the rose family. The shiny 5–7-lobed leaves are apple-green, a lovely contrast to the scarlet berries when they come in autumn. And it can be planted in any position and will tolerate all types of soil from limy to acid, moist or dry, but does not

12 *Cotoneaster frigidus*: Himalayan Tree-cotoneaster

like a very humid atmosphere. The berries are always a good food supply for birds in winter.

A may with an intensely red double flower is a variety of the slightly less common Midland or English Hawthorn, *C. oxyacantha*, and named 'Paul's Scarlet' or 'Coccinea Plena'. Though it is usually a smaller tree than the Common Hawthorn, I have a fully grown specimen some 30 ft (10 m) tall at the corner of my garden, which makes a glorious sight at the end of May, a veritable crimson cloud. These trees only just flower in the month of May to justify their name, because they were used for spring festivals under the Old Style calendar, which ran twelve days later than the dates of the present day. Unfortunately, these lovely blooms are sterile, so the tree does not set any fruit.

There are several other species that make very handsome garden trees and I mention one or two that I think are the choicest. *C. crus-galli*, the Cockspur Thorn from the St Lawrence river in Canada, south into North America, Zone 4, is an attractive tree, usually growing wider than it is tall, but with fearsome thorns which can be 3 in (8 cm) long, gradually becoming branched spines. So for a garden specimen I would choose the form *C. crus-galli pyracanthifolia* which is practically thornless and does not reach more than 15 ft (5 m), becoming a very elegant specimen when mature and forming a perfect umbrella shape. From the horizontal branches the leaves hang glossy and dark green, narrower than the oval ones of the type, and turning scarlet in the autumn.

Another useful thornless species is the Tansy-leaved Thorn, *C. tanacetifolia*, with such an attractive common name and soft grey downy leaves. It makes quite a slow-growing tree — is originally from Asia Minor — and has fragrant white flowers in June and large yellow fruits with the delicious scent and flavour of apples.

The Red Haw or Downy Hawthorn, *C. mollis*, is a native of Central North America, and is also grown in Europe for its pleasing flowers which come in June and are white with a red and yellow centre. The leaves, 4 in (10 cm) long and nearly as wide, and the large round fruit in September, are both downy; but unfortunately the thorns are 2 in (5 cm) long, so it needs siting carefully.

All these hawthorns will tolerate Zone 4 but a very desirable and a slightly more tender one is *C. azarolus*, the Azarole or Mediterranean Medlar. The flowers, grouped as 3 in (8 cm) clusters in June, are a little larger, pure-white with mauve anthers, followed by the larger fruits which can be yellowy-orange or red, or even in one form creamy-white when ripe. The leaves are deeply cut, shiny above and downy beneath. On this species there are strange moss-like bracts at the base of the fruit. Against a warm protected wall this tree would be a choice one to grow, for the fruits are used in the Mediterranean to make jam and as a flavouring for liqueurs.

There are not nearly so many hawthorns found in Asia as in America — in fact, none comes from Japan — but there is a very decorative small tree from north-east Asia, *C. pinnatifida*, with large glossy leaves 4 in (10 cm) long with two lobes at either side of the base and a very long stalk. The sweet crimson fruit is spotted, yet good to eat. The white flowers are ¾ in (2 cm) across. An even more stunning variety, from Northern China, is *C. pinnatifida major* with larger gleaming red berries and the toothed leaves turning brilliantly crimson in autumn. Another bonus is that it does not have any, or many, thorns to speak of and will tolerate Zone 5.

My favourite is the Glastonbury Thorn, *C. monogyna* 'Biflora' ('Praecox'), for its legendary name and the fact that it flowers in mild winters, sometimes before Christmas, the leaves also appearing early.

Propagation is by seed, but patience is needed, as this takes two years to germinate successfully. Grafting or budding is best for the varieties.

DAVIDIA

Davidia involucrata has the charming names of the Pocket-Handkerchief, Dove or Ghost tree because when the large white bracts, their veins tinged green, hang from the branches in May they certainly do look like these objects somehow lodged among the leaves. In the centre of the two bracts, one wider and longer than the other, is a boss of the inconspicuous flowers. These produce fruit like little green pears which, by the end of the summer, have turned purple, enclosing a seed like a nut. If you have the space, this is an easy and unusual-looking tree to grow in any good soil, as long as it is not too dry. It will make a nice specimen on the lawn given some shade, as the base of the trunk does not like to have too much sun. So the edge of woodland in dappled shade gives ideal conditions. A friend of mine has a tree growing in just such a woodland setting, and it flowers spectactularly well.

This tree is quite hardy to Zone 6, and very attractive with its unusually bright green leaves, nicely rounded with a pointed tip and up to 5 in (12 cm) in length. The variety *D. involucrata vilmoriniana* has been found to be even hardier, to Zone 5, but otherwise is very similar, except the leaves are smooth not hairy underneath and the fruits a slightly different rounder shape. Unfortunately, it does not flower when very young, so you must wait for the lovely sight of your handkerchief tree, but the wait will definitely be worthwhile.

DRIMYS

Drimys is a genus of some 40 species, in the magnolia family, and from different parts of the world; but the one, *D. winteri* that grows to tree-size, 8–25 ft (2.5–8 m) tall, comes from Chile and Argentina. It is known as Winter's Bark, and this is made into a substitute for cinnamon, and was once drunk as a tonic; the seed pods, when dried, are used as a pepper substitute.

The long-stalked bunches of fragrant white flowers with their golden stamens are carried all over the tree, set against the large narrow gleaming leaves, very aromatic when bruised. To avoid the habit of many of the magnolia species, keep the trunk to a single stem by careful pruning and then it will quickly develop into a handsome tree with the upper branches laden with blossom in May. It is a little slow to bloom when young but being a fast-grower it will soon reach flowering size. The variety *D. winteri latifolia* is even more desirable, having larger leaves and flowers, and it has been found to be slightly hardier.

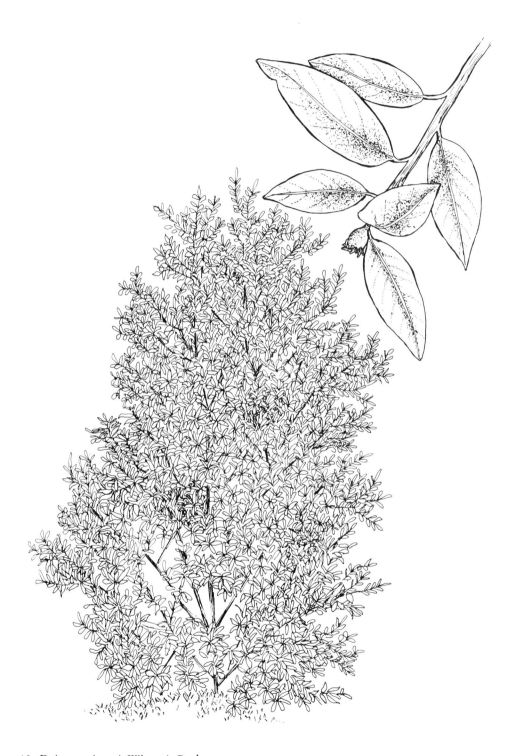

13 *Drimys winteri*: Winter's Bark

ELAEAGNUS

The elaeagnus family consists of both deciduous and evergreen species and most of them make handsome shrubs; but there are two that grow to make good-sized trees, both of these being deciduous.

The name elaeagnus is an old Greek one for the willow — and the one I grow certainly does resemble the willow-leaved pear — and also from elaios, an olive, from the berry that forms following the blooming of the small but nicely scented fuchsia-like flowers. My *E. angustifolia*, commonly known as the Oleaster or Russian Olive, has made a 20 ft (6 m) tree, and tolerates any sea gales with no ill-effects. The leaves are small and greeny-silver, the blooms along the spiny stems being a furry yellow in clusters, followed by oval amber fruits. I prune it back against the fence to stop it shading surrounding shrubs and I think it would make a very suitable tree for the small garden, especially if any untoward growth is pruned away regularly. And these trees are very hardy, tolerating Zone 2.

The second one that makes a nice tree size is *E. umbellata*, the Chinese Silverberry or Wild Olive, and this flowers a little earlier, in May. It does not grow quite so tall but is more spreading in habit. In autumn it really lives up to its name by producing silvery balls of fruit, which gradually turn a soft red, a nice contrast against the leaves.

These elaeagnus trees will grow happily in a dry situation in any reasonable soil that is not too chalky, and they can be propagated by seed in February.

The *E. umbellata* comes from Japan, while *E. angustifolia* is found in the temperate areas of Europe and Asia.

EMBOTHRIUM

The embothrium thrives in woodland conditions which give dappled but not too much shade, such as in a clearing; and with moist soil for its roots, *E. coccineum* is a startling tree to grow. Composed of only a few forms in the genus, they are natives of Chile and are only happy in Zone 8 and therefore need the warmth of the southern parts of Great Britain, doing particularly well in the south-western regions and in the same parts of Eire. There they will thrive and grow quickly to become a tall tree. So, in spite of being known as the Chilean Fire Bush, in a favoured site it will reach tree size, of upright habit, attaining 20–30 ft (6–10 m) in around 20 years.

The ideal soil is sandy peat, as it is not happy in alkaline conditions and also needs good drainage. The flowers are fiery-scarlet, orange-tinted, and resembling those of the honeysuckle, the leaves oval and a rich shining green. But in the best and hardiest variety, *E. coccineum lanceolatum*, where the leaves are lance-shaped as the name implies, the blooms are massed up the stems making a blaze of colour when the tree flowers in May and June. And the best form of this is known as Norquinco Valley.

There is a variety, *E. coccineum longifolium*, with slimmer and longer leaves which will remain on the tree throughout the year, whereas *E. coccineum*

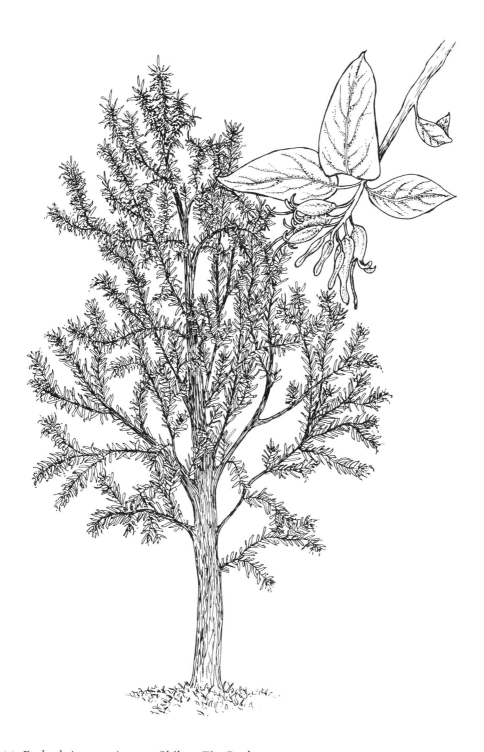

14 *Embothrium coccineum*: Chilean Fire Bush

lanceolatum is often partly deciduous; of course, this depends very much on the amount of protection provided.

There is a beautiful well-grown specimen of this flamboyant tree planted in a protected woodland garden two miles (3 km) inland from me, but it is in a reasonably open position by the drive, with the chance of plenty of sun and yet with the background of other trees and shrubs to give it shelter.

EUCALYPTUS

The eucalyptus, Gum Tree or Ironbark Tree is evergreen and a member of the myrtle family. Though there are over 500 species, most of them are not frost-hardy, being natives of Australia, and they particularly dislike cold winds. They grow so fast — up to 6 ft (2 m) a year — that a strong bitter wind will whip them over and break their tender young trunks and brown their elegant aromatic leaves before they have had time to get established. For this reason they are best pruned hard for the first few springs, cutting at least a third away, so that the main stem is encouraged to thicken and strengthen.

Two that are reasonably hardy in Southern England and Zone 6 (though really preferring Zone 7) are *E. gunnii*, the Cider Gum from South Australia and Tasmania; and *E. dalrympleana*. In *E. gunnii* the leaves of the young trees are a very attractive circular disk shape, blue with an iridescent sheen. When they age they change shape and colour completely, becoming nearly 4 in (10 cm) long, shaped like a sickle, narrow, curved and pointed and sage-green. *E. gunnii* will make a tall tree sometimes to 60–70 ft (18–20 m), but if pruned every year will form an elegant bush, and in this case you will retain mostly the interesting disc-shaped young leaves. The flowers come very late in the summer, a year after the buds have first formed, puffs of white with yellow stamens in bunches of three, followed by bell-like fruits.

E. dalrympleana is smaller but faster-growing, making a nice conical shape. It has an attractive marbled bark, which strips off, except at the very base of the trunk, revealing smooth white areas. The young leaves are copper-coloured and turn a greenish-grey as they mature; they are long like a scimitar. In fact, the leaves can be various shapes in different species, from heart-shaped to spear-shaped, usually with smooth margins.

In sub-tropical areas of the world one of the most stunning eucalyptus is the Red-flowering Gum, *E. ficifolia*, a small round-headed slow-growing tree native to a coastal area of South West Australia. The shining green leaves make a wonderful setting for the flame of the blooms, which can be as much as seven on a long stalk; their colour comes, actually, from the filaments of the stamens. Unfortunately it is so tender, needing Zone 10, that it can only be grown in a conservatory in Britain. Some of these species are wonderfully adapted to survive destruction by drought or fire by possessing a lignotuber, unlike any other tree in the world. This is a bulb-like growth which forms just below the level of the ground and stores nutrients for drought, and enables it to rejuvenate after forest fires. The trees are best planted in the spring so that they have the summer to get established and, as they do not transplant well, it is best to keep them in their pots until their permanent position has been decided.

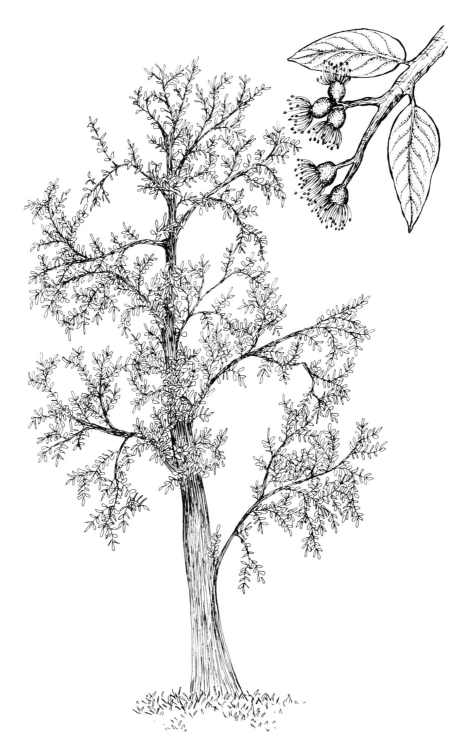

15 *Eucalyptus gunnii*: Cider Gum

Eucalyptus propagate easily and quickly from seed sown under glass in the spring and often grow far more rapidly from seedlings than from large container-grown plants. But grafting is best when you want to retain the same flower colour, as this can vary when grown from seed. Several oils are produced from these trees and where they grow prolifically their abundant flowers are a great source of honey.

They will flourish in all types of well-drained soil, except a very chalky one. But if you have that type of ground, there is one eucalyptus, *E. parvifolia*, which thrives on chalk and yet will tolerate quite severe winters. A medium-height tree with narrow greenish-blue leaves and smooth grey bark.

Eucalyptus are best planted alone in full sun, perhaps in the shelter of a fairly distant belt of trees which will temper the worst winds, as they resent being too near other plants.

EUCRYPHIA

Eucryphias are a small genus of about six species with various attractive hybrids and I think they are very desirable trees to grow. To see one in full flower in the month of August, when the first flush of summer flowering is beginning, gives a singular pleasure. It makes a very good specimen for the garden as it is slow-growing, and most of the trees are columnar in shape and the blooms cover the whole plant with their white cup-shaped flowers and striking purple anthers against the background of rich green leaves.

Ecryphias prefer an acid to neutral soil, well-drained, and the roots shaded, with the tree in sun. I have a plant now 15 ft (5 m) high growing in a clay soil, but well-drained as it is on a slope, and I think it likes this position. Surrounded by a rowan and a philadelphus tree, so that it is shaded from the hot summer sun, in winter when the two neighbouring trees are leafless, it gets plenty of light, sun and air to ripen the wood for the next summer's flowers.

In these apparently ideal surrounding conditions, it seems to tolerate the slightly adverse soil. But the hybrid I planted is *E.* × *intermedia*, a cross between *E. glutinosa* and *E. lucida*, and the one that seems to be most tolerant of limy soil.

Look out for this spectacular tree flowering in some of the famous gardens; it is a sight worth seeing when a 20 ft (6 m) or more tree towering above you is covered from head to foot in the delicate white flowers, such a fine contrast to the dark green, shiny, usually evergreen leaves. And in a mild autumn the flowers will continue till December before the first frost touches and browns their whiteness.

These trees come from Chile or Tasmania and two of the loveliest crosses were raised in the British Isles. *E* × *intermedia*, with its free-flowering form 'Rostrevor', were raised in Northern Ireland; perhaps the choicest one of all, *E.* × *nymansensis* 'Nymansay', a more rapid grower, with larger flowers some 2½ in (6 cm) across, was raised in Sussex. *E. glutinosa*, which is deciduous unlike the other varieties, has an attractive display in autumn when the leaves turn a glowing red.

Though these trees are a little tender, being happiest in Zone 7, they are worth trying in a sheltered corner, for they make a beautiful and unusual addition to the variety of plants you can have in your garden.

Eucryphias are best propagated from seed, sown in a mixture of peat and sand in February or March when they will germinate easily. If they are nursed through the early years they can eventually be planted in their permanent position and by then will prove remarkably hardy. Layering is another method of propagation which is fairly successful, but cuttings seem very difficult to root. They require no pruning, save for the occasional removal of any dead wood.

EUODIA

The euodia, sometimes spelt evodia, is a genus consisting of evergreen and deciduous trees and shrubs with both simple and compound leaves. The trees are deciduous and belong to the rue family, and they are also related to that of the citrus. There are three species that grow well in any type of soil and make decorative small trees, if given plenty of sun.

The first, which comes from China, is *E. hupehensis*, with large compound glossy leaves and flattish heads of white flowers in mid-summer rather like the viburnum, followed, on female trees, by crimson fruits. This species will even do well in poor chalky soil.

The second is *E. velutina* which makes a smaller, less spreading tree, with pinnate leaves and shoots which are covered in a velvety down — as its name implies. In August and September the umbels of whitish-yellow blooms appear at every leaf axil — usually on only the current year's shoots — and make it the most attractive of the three for the garden.

The third one, *E. daniellii*, is also known as the Korean Euodia and it comes from both North China and Korea. It is fast-growing with large pinnate leaves and strongly-scented heads of matt-white flowers, as much as 6 in (15 cm) across, in August and September. The fruits which develop from them are maroon-black capsules with a hooked point. The leaves turn a soft butter-yellow in early winter.

These graceful trees are quite hardy in Zone 5, but in very cold areas it helps to choose a site which is not too exposed, especially in the case of *E. velutina*.

FAGUS

Beeches are one of the prime tree species, being a genus of only ten, and belonging to the same family as the oak. Some of them grow to a great height, well over 100 ft (30 m), and a beech wood is a magnificent sight, providing such a dense canopy in summer that little else thrives below, especially as it is shallow-rooted. Yet in winter the bare branches form a delicate outline against the sky with their slim pointed buds. It is a tree grown north of the Equator, the *Nothofagus* being found in the southern hemisphere. Beeches are deciduous and very easy as to soil, being tolerant of chalk as long as it is well-drained, though the American Beech is not quite so adaptable and does not thrive where there is lime in the soil.

The Common Beech, *F. sylvatica*, is a native of Europe and Zone 4 and though it does reach great heights, it has many varieties and cultivars which are more suitable for the average garden. However, the beech itself does make a very attractive hedge if regularly pruned. In early May the fresh green alternate leaves appear downy and soft with well-marked veins. These become golden-brown in autumn, stiff and crackly, usually remaining in place all winter, particularly if the hedge is pruned in mid-summer, and only falling off when the new leaves appear. So although it is a deciduous tree these dead leaves make the hedge a very attractive feature all the year, and provide shelter for surrounding plants. In full-grown trees the branches come well up the trunk giving a very pleasant grove effect in woods and forests; and a single tree in a garden can provide delightfully light shade if any low-growing branches are cut away, as a specimen tree tends to produce these to protect its smooth grey bark from unwelcome sunlight. The carpet of leaves which eventually builds up beneath their canopy makes marvellous compost, when well rotted down, as it is rich in potash.

At the same time as the leaves, the catkins appear, the male flowers grouped together hanging on long stalks, and the female come on the same tree but separately in bunches of two or three, which become the familiar nuts covered by a woody husk, 4-lobed with prickles. These triangular nuts, usually two, are edible and known as mast. They are much enjoyed by animals, though at one time they were a source of food for humans, yielding an oil which was made into margarine in Germany during the two World Wars. The flowers of *F. sylvatica* appear in May and the nuts are ripe by late September.

Two with most pleasingly coloured leaves are *F. sylvatica purpurea*, the Purple Beech, and *F. sylvatica* 'Cuprea', the Copper Beech, with a browner tone to the leaves. There are several other forms, one of the strongest colours being produced by *F. sylvatica* 'Riversii', a rich deep purple. Then there is the Weeping Beech, *F. sylvatica* 'Pendula', which grows to a fair size, with branches of green leaves sweeping to the ground; when strategically placed, this graceful tree can be a focal point of the garden. But it does become quite large and in a more confined space or garden *F. sylvatica* 'Purpurea Pendula', the Weeping Purple Beech, would be the best one to choose. And try to select a sunny site for the coloured-leaved beeches; not only do they thrive but the sun on their leaves makes them look even more attractive. There is a very good yellow-leaved variety, the Golden Beech, *F. sylvatica* 'Zlatia', with buttery leaves which turn green and then become yellow again in the autumn. This is a slow-growing form and would make an excellent contrast to the green and purple beeches in a planting scheme. But if the garden design requires a slender tree, there is the choice of *F. sylvatica* 'Dawyck', a pillar of green leaves which turn a brownish-gold in autumn, the columnar shape broadening a little with age; or *F. sylvatica* 'Aurea Pendula' with chrome-yellow foliage, growing tall yet slim, as the branches hang practically parallel to the trunk. The flowers and fruit of the purple beeches are tinged with pink, making these trees even more delightful.

The American Beech, *F. grandifolia* from eastern North America, and growing to an attractive pyramid shape, does not make such a large specimen in

6 *Arbutus unedo*: Strawberry Tree

7 *Catalpa speciosa*: Western Catalpa

England, though it is hardier to Zone 3. The bark is more silvery than the grey of *F. sylvatica*, with dark markings; and the leaves are slimmer, longer and more pointed with more veins and toothed edges, a paler green underneath than above, turning a soft brown in autumn. And it spreads by root suckering, except where the tree is one grafted on to *F. sylvatica*. Before the passenger pigeon was shot to extinction, great flocks of these birds came to the forests of American Beech to roost and feed.

Beech wood has many uses, principally for fuel, but also in the making of furniture and flooring.

Propagation is by grafting, or from seed by planting the nuts in autumn; or by rooted suckers in the case of the American Beech, as I have mentioned.

FRAXINUS

The Ash or Fraxinus is a genus of about 70 species, most of them forming large trees which grow very quickly, so they would tend to crowd a small garden and are better given plenty of space. But in the right situation they are a tough and useful tree, being very tolerant of strong winds and sea-spray.

F. excelsior, the Common Ash or European Ash and hardy in Zone 3, is such a vigorous grower that it is best planted in parks and very large gardens, where it likes deep cool soil and will grow well on chalk. It is a common sight all over Europe with its slender deeply indented reddish-brown trunk, which is smooth and grey when young, and from which very good quality timber is obtained, pale and pliable, but strong. The compound pinnate leaves appear in late May, some time after the flowers, and are a rich green, turning a butter-yellow in autumn as they fall. The inconspicuous greeny-yellow flowers, the stamens red, are produced in fluffy clusters. This tree will reach 130 ft (40 m), but there are varieties which are smaller and slower in growth and could be planted in a large garden, as long as they are not placed near the house or any walls.

A variety known as the Golden Ash, *F. excelsior* 'Jaspidea', is a magnificent sight when its leaves turn a soft yellow in autumn, and the young twigs and branches in winter are also golden, a nice contrast against the dark grey trunk. Look for the one with the alternative name 'Aurea' which is slow-growing and should not get too big for a decent-sized garden.

F. velutina, the Arizona Ash or Velvet Ash, makes a light airy tree, and is a native of North Mexico and the south-western parts of the United States, and Zone 5. The male and female flowers are on separate trees whereas with the European Ash the flowers may be on different trees or the same tree or even together in one flower. The leaves are much smaller, turning yellow in autumn, with only 3–5 leaflets and downy, as are the young velvety shoots — hence its name — and the dark grey bark is deeply furrowed. In winter the buds are brown. It is very tolerant of alkaline soils and can withstand great variations in temperature. In very dry areas its bark has a silvery sheen, and it does best in the eastern half of England rather than the warmer, damper south-west. Its timber is not as strong as other ashes.

Another ash that does better in drier areas is *F. oxycarpa*, a compact grower and slender when young, not reaching much above 30 ft (10 m) a little shorter than *F. velutina*. The glossy green leaves are smaller, but in the variety *F. oxycarpa* 'Raywood', the Claret Ash, they have a blue tinge and change to a rich maroon in autumn, giving a splendid show — the following winter buds being brown.

In North America there are variations of the Common Ash, white, red and green, which contribute greatly to the colourful display in that country. Unfortunately, most of these are too large for the average garden, but make excellent trees, with their elegant rounded shape, for lining the streets, both in America and Europe.

But I think the choicest to grow is one of the flowering species of the Ornus group, *F. ornus*, the Manna Ash from Southern Europe and Zone 5, which makes a denser crown and rarely exceeds 30 ft (10 m) in height. It produces delightful massed clusters of matt-white scented flowers in May, with showy petals, unlike most ashes. The fruits are brownish-red and winged, with just one seed. The pinnate bright green young leaves have 5–9 leaflets, toothed and sometimes not all of the same shape. This Flowering Ash has a smooth grey bark and grey winter buds and is known as manna for the sap which is tapped by an incision in the bark; this sugary substance is cooked and used medicinally, often as a mild laxative, particularly in southern Italy.

Both *F. ornus* and *F. oxycarpa* are particularly sun-loving. The ash needs little pruning but the Ornus group can have crowded growths thinned.

Propagate by seed taken from the tree, but the ash, like the sycamore, is notorious for scattering its seeds everywhere and these can be troublesome, as they grow quickly, unless they are potted up and moved to a suitable site. The garden varieties, especially *F. ornus*, are better grafted.

GINKGO

The *Ginkgo biloba* is a very ancient tree, the last survivor of the genus, and the form of the leaves gives it the name of the Maidenhair Tree from their likeness to the fern of the same name. The name Ginkgo is from the Japanese and should really have been correctly transcribed as Ginkyo. From the sight of this graceful deciduous tree you would never think it was actually a conifer in origin, though its ancestry is now thought to be even more remote. The curious leaves are fan-shaped, divided into two lobes, a lovely glossy green, turning to a lemon-yellow before they fall.

The male of the species is the better one to grow, as the shape is less spreading and also the yellow catkins, though reluctant to appear, are more desirable when they do, for the female flowers produce fruit which have an unpleasant smell. The ginkgo is easy to grow in any climate to Zone 4, tolerating any soil, even in industrial sites, and growing 10 ft (3 m) in ten years. These trees line a street in Washington and there is a very beautiful specimen to be seen in Kew Gardens, the bark tinged with red.

For the smaller garden the best variety to plant would be *G. biloba* 'Fastigiata' or 'Tremonia', columnar and conical in shape. And a weeping form *G. biloba* 'Pendula' gives a particularly dramatic effect as the bright green leaves turn yellow.

16 *Ginkgo biloba*: Maidenhair Tree

GLEDITSIA

Gleditsias are very beautiful foliage trees to have in the garden, but unless you have plenty of space for them, with their graceful pinnate or bipinnate leaves, beware of the ones that have fearsome spikes on their trunks and branches, as these can be as much as 1 ft (30 cm) long.

The gleditsia is a genus of about a dozen deciduous species belonging to the pea family. The slow-growing *G. japonica* is one of the best smaller forms with its pinnate sprays of green fern-like leaves, and its pyramidal shape. The bell-like yellowy-green male and female blooms appear on the same tree in June, the trunk being liberally covered in spines. This tree will tolerate Zone 5; slightly more tender, requiring Zone 6, is *G. caspica*, the Caspian Locust, which makes a charming small tree, with the largest leaflets, but producing the most vicious spikes, as it ages, of all the gleditsias.

G. triacanthos, the Honey Locust, is perhaps the species most commonly seen, as it will tolerate Zone 4. It comes from the central and eastern areas of the United States, and Ontario in Canada, where it reaches a great height. It is frequently planted in the southern parts of England and France, where it is usually seen around 20–35 ft (6–10.5 m).

Some varieties of this species have no deadly spines, and yet are just as decorative. *G. triancanthos* 'Moraine', the Morain Locust, is fast-growing, but although the flowers are similar to those of *G. japonica*, it does not have fruits, or its pyramid shape, nor the clouds of tiny leaflets, but develops into a much more broadly branched tree with no thorns. *G. triacanthos* 'Shademaster' grows even faster than the Morain and *G. triacanthos* 'Ruby Lace' has rather spectacular young red shoots. A weeping form, *G. triacanthos* 'Bujoti' ('Pendula'), makes a very attractive small bushy tree, the slim hanging branches clothed in a mass of narrow leaflets.

But *G. triacanthos inermis* is the variety to plant if you intend to use it for a shade tree, as it is ideal for this with its delicate feathery foliage which gives dappled protection in an area where you may want to sit, and on lawns the light foliage does not damage the grass when it falls in autumn, and this tree does not cast too much gloom if planted near the house. Also, when they are in some shade themselves, the thorny varieties do not seem to produce their vicious spines so prolifically, which is a distinct advantage; though they do, as a whole, prefer to be in full sun. *G. triacanthos* 'Inermis Aurea', known also as *G. triacanthos* 'Sunburst', is a cheerful sight with its young leaves of a chrome-yellow all the year from spineless stems, the older foliage becoming green, so making it one of the most desirable thornless ones to give bright colour to the garden.

The greenish flowers of the gleditsias are fragrant and prolific, though relatively small; but the pods which follow the blooms are not. They are very long and thin, as much as 15 in (38 cm) in the case of *G. triacanthos*, curved like a scimitar, brown and gleaming; with *G. triacanthos inermis* they are a little shorter with a reddish tinge. They show up brilliantly when the leaves of this Honey Locust turn yellow in the autumn, having been a fresh green in spring

17 *Gleditsia japonica*

and gradually turning darker with a blue gleam to them, then finally becoming yellow before they drop. The leaves appear late and fall early, so their season is short, but the pods remain on the trees till December. Their name is explained by the yellow substance that lines the walls of the pods, which has a sweet flavour remindful of honey.

Should you want a slow-growing variety of *G. triacanthos*, the cultivar 'Elegantissima' has a neat habit and rarely grows more than 15 ft (5 m), so it would be very suitable for a restricted space or in a small garden, with its large, mimosa-like leaves.

Gleditsias will grow happily in any soil as long as it is well-drained; and if you wish to propagate them, sow seed in the spring with glass protection.

Being such tolerant trees, they make ideal planting in cities, where there may be atmospheric pollution, and they will also stand up well to dry or very windy conditions.

HALESIA

The halesias are a small genus of trees, found mostly in North America. *H. carolina (tetraptera)*, with the lovely name of the Snowdrop Tree, flowers in April or May before the leaves. The drooping pure-white flowers hang in lateral fascicles of eight or ten along the branches. So the most effective way to plant this tree is in a position where it can be viewed from below. Then the full beauty of the blooms can be seen and appreciated. When the leaves appear they are toothed and oval; later on there are 4-winged seeds. As its name implies this species is a native of the river banks of North Carolina, in Britain it will grow to around 15–20 ft (5–6 m).

H. monticola, the hardiest of the species at Zone 5, though most will tolerate Zone 4 to 5, makes a bigger tree, faster growing, and comes from the high hills of the south-east in the United States. Here it grows wild and is called the Mountain Snowdrop Tree or Mountain Silverbell, though in the British Isles it will not grow as tall as in its native habitat. The correspondingly larger blooms of this tree are more than 1 in (2.5 cm) long and delicately veined. The variety *H. monticola* 'Rosea' has flowers of the palest pink.

But perhaps the best variety of this species is *H. monticola vestita* with the largest white blooms, occasionally with a touch of pink, the light green leaves having soft hairs at first; these disappear with age, leaving the leaf glabrous, and becoming yellow before falling.

The green fruits remain on the tree right through the winter and are often still there when the new season's flowers come.

The soil for halesias should be acid, so light peaty ground is ideal. However, it is said by some experts that *H. carolina* is not so fussy as to soil, and will grow on lime, if peat or good compost is well-mixed in, too. So there is a good choice for whichever kind of ground you have in your garden.

Propagation is best by sowing ripe seed in the autumn, or by layering, or taking cuttings in spring.

HAMAMELIS

Hamamelis, the Witch Hazel, is a deciduous genus of about six species, most of them shrubs or shrubby in habit, but two do attain tree-size, and have very elegant and decorative flowers and leaves for the garden, especially as they are in bloom during the winter, when many other trees are bare or at rest.

H. mollis, the most commonly grown Witch Hazel, does become quite tall, but is too bushy to be called a tree, never reaching much above 7–9 ft (2–3 m), though it does have the strongest scented flowers. But *H. virginiana* from North America and Zone 4 can reach 15 ft (5 m) or more. This is the first of the species to flower, in September to November, which has the drawback in that the flowers are hidden by the leaves, which have not yet fallen. These curious spidery blooms, golden-yellow, have a sweet, though faint, scent. The leaves are sharply oval-shaped, toothed, and hairy on the stalk and undersides. These turn golden, too, in the autumn which is an added reason why the flowers are rather difficult to see. This species is the source of the well-known fluid used as a remedy for bruising and to staunch bleeding, the oil for it being extracted from the bark.

More flamboyant is the *H. japonica* 'Arborea' from Japan which flowers from December to March with the fragrant tawny-yellow blooms, touched with claret at the base, strung along the bare branches. This species will grow to 25 ft (8 m) or more and displays well when grown against an east or north wall, as its branches grow horizontally and can be fanned out and tied along the wall, the little flowers grouped in dense clusters. The leaves are shiny and rather diamond in shape and become a rich yellow in autumn. As a free-standing specimen it will develop a broad crown, but the important thing to remember is the background for these Witch Hazels so that the unusual curly flower-petals can show up to the best advantage. A white wall or red brick or dark evergreen foliage are all effective. The variety *H. japonica flavopurpurascens* has a similar habit to 'Arborea' and red-based chrome-yellow flowers.

Hamamelis grows happily in sun or half-shade; it likes a deep rich soil, well-drained, and acid to neutral, not chalky, though it will tolerate a certain amount of lime. I have a plant which thrives on my clay soil, but I give it plenty of peat and compost.

Propagate by layering or grafting; though they produce two gleaming black seeds from the fruit capsule, these take a very long time to germinate, and the colours of the progeny can vary a good deal.

HOHERIA

Hoheria is a very beautiful tree from the mallow family which, like the eucryphia, starts to flower around August. I first read about this tree years ago when its merits were praised, by the famous gardener Vita Sackville West, in an article where she mentioned that she grew it in her garden at Sissinghurst Castle in Kent. I wrote to her and she told me where to buy the tree and I planted the species *H. lyallii* (also known as *Plagianthus lyallii* or *Gaya lyallii*), against a

18 *Hoheria sextylosa*

potting shed wall and it grew fast and produced its clusters of lovely white flowers — like cherry blossom — for many years. Eventually a particularly severe winter killed the poor thing off, for its ideal Zone is 7. However, with wall protection from cold winds and reasonable winters, it can certainly be grown successfully in the South of England where the Zone is 6–7.

There is a very magnificent specimen of *H. sexstylosa*, at least 45 ft (13.5 m) tall, and reputed to be the tallest in Southern England, growing in West Sussex. This was damaged by recent cold winters, but has survived, unlike my tree, so it is possibly hardier, or the position it is growing in is more favourable than the one I gave mine. *H. lyallii* has smooth leaves which become hairy and grey as they age, whereas *H. sexstylosa* has slimmer leaves, serrated and bright green.

Another attractive species is *H. glabrata* which blooms earlier than the other two, in June or July, producing the largest flowers, fragrant and almost transparently white, with sharp yellow stamens.

These trees come from both islands of New Zealand and the genus consists of five species with several cultivars and all are easy as to soil.

They are mostly deciduous, sometimes retaining their leaves in a favoured position. But I recommend them as a beautiful tree to try, even if you only succeed in keeping it, with its delicate flowers and interesting leaves, in your garden for a year or so. You can always take cuttings of the unripened wood to grow on in safety, so that you can replace your tree if you should be so unfortunate as to lose it in a bad winter; or layering is another method that produces successful progeny. Because of their place of origin, they are more likely to thrive where there are maritime conditions.

IDESIA

There is only one species in the genus of idesia, and it has two other forms, but it is an extremely decorative deciduous tree to have in the garden in winter. The very pale green deliciously fragrant female flowers appear in early summer, having no petals but around half a dozen sepals; the male flower has a greater number of stamens but no fruits to follow. These appear on the female trees, like a bunch of grapes, in graceful drooping racemes of scarlet berries the size of small peas, which remain on the tree after the fall of the leaves, gradually turning a brownish-red. These ovate leaves are bright green with long and conspicuous crimson footstalks; the leaves are often 4 in (10 cm) across and glaucous beneath, of an elegant heart shape.

Both sexes of this tree must be planted to obtain fruit, and even then the tree needs a good sunny summer to produce the clusters of berries which are so attractive. It grows to about 20 ft (6 m) but there are trees in Southern England that are known to be higher than this. This is in the area of Zone 6, which is the lowest temperature it will tolerate. A woodland setting with other trees and shrubs nearby gives an ideal environment for the well-drained but moisture-retaining soil it requires, ideally neutral towards acid, deep and rich.

I. polycarpa is a native of China and Japan and the form *I. polycarpa vestita* from Western China is slightly hardier and, instead of a bloom beneath the leaves, these are covered with fine hairs. *I. polycarpa crispa* is a distinct form with leaves curiously crisped and cut.

The idesia is easy to propagate from seed, but the only method of obtaining the sex of the plant required is by cleft grafting, with male scion on female stock.

A really interesting tree to grow, with its horizontal branches and thick pithy young shoots, even though it is necessary to wait several years for the idesia to flower.

ILEX

The holly or ilex consists of a large genus of around 300 shrubs and trees and, together with the Scotch fir, they are among the oldest trees we have in Britain. The deciduous varieties are not grown very often, but they do have striking fruits, *I. macrocarpa* perhaps being the most desirable with its serrated leaves, at least 5 in (12 cm) long, and black cherry-like fruits.

It is rather pleasant to have a holly tree in your garden, especially if it produces its lovely red berries for house decoration at Christmas, but do plant it well away from the house, for although slow-growing it will reach a good height in time and, apart from dominating with its shade, the prickly leaves of many of the varieties which fall from time to time — even on evergreens as they renew themselves — are unpleasant to come across when weeding nearby or walking barefoot. Some distance from the house it makes a handsome backcloth and a lovely sight with its dark shining green leaves.

Although both male and female trees have fragrant white flowers, you normally need to have either kind planted near each other to get berries, which incidentally are poisonous. But some of the varieties have practically spineless leaves and *I. × altaclarensis* 'Camelliifolia' is particularly desirable, growing into a pyramid shape which is very attractive for your garden design and producing from purple stems leaves of a similar colour which gradually turn a rich dark green. The berries are large, red and prolific.

Should you prefer yellow berries, *I. aquifolium* 'Bacciflava' is the one to choose; it does have spiny leaves, but they make a nice foil for the golden berries.

One of the best weeping forms is *I. aquifolium* 'Argentea Pendula', known as Perry's Silver Weeping Holly. It gradually forms a dome of white-edged dark green leaves to the ground and covered eventually with bright red berries.

There are several hollies with varigated leaves, one of the choicest being *I. aquifolium* 'Madame Briot', the green leaves from purple stems being brightly edged with yellow. It produces a fine crop of berries, and makes a good barrier near the edges of the garden, as the leaves are unusually spiny.

But two of the best fruiting hollies are self-fertile, so if you only have room for one holly tree, choose *I. aquifolium* 'J. C. van Tol' or 'Pyramidalis'. Their bright green leaves from green stems are practically without spines and they produce an abundance of berries even in a poor year.

I have mentioned a few of the hollies I like, but the choice is so great it is best to go to a large nursery where you can see the numerous kinds offered and select the one most suitable for the position you have allocated for it. Standards and half-standards are very attractive and those with sharp spines can be planted and kept trimmed with secateurs as a tall barrier hedge. For these trees are easy as to soil, and will withstand city pollution and salty sea-winds, in any situation; but in total shade they will not produce a good show of berries. There are several that need some protection, originating from Zones 6–8, but the main group is very hardy, tolerating Zone 5.

An exciting orange-berried one, *I. aquifolium* 'Amber', found by chance as a seedling in a hedge at a famous nursery, has recently been awarded a First Class Certificate by the Royal Horticultural Society, and sounds well worth having.

The North American hollies differ slightly from the English ones, some requiring an acid soil and also the berries are formed on the present year's growth. With the English holly they are produced on last year's shoots.

I have found these trees make good strong frames up which to grow a rambler rose or a clematis. In this way you get two flowerings from both plants in the same area of the garden.

ITEA

The itea or Sweetspire is a slim graceful small tree rarely reaching more than 6–8 ft (2–2.5 m) and resembling a willow in form, the name itea being the old Greek word for willow. The more common form of the two most widely grown from this small genus is *I. ilicifolia*, an evergreen from China resembling a holly with glossy green leaves. But from July to August it has beautiful racemes of yellow-green flowers, nearly 12 in (30 cm) long and sweetly scented. Though it is not particularly tender, because of its delicate habit it is best grown against or near a wall, far enough away to allow plenty of moisture, as it does not like to be dry at the roots but it does like a sunny position.

The deciduous variety from Virginia, USA, *I. virginica*, has a more upright habit of growth and the fragrant racemes of bloom are also upright and creamy in colour. This is more shrub-like and only reaches around 5 ft (1.5 m), but if you require a deciduous little tree in a certain place in the garden, it is a slightly unusual plant and the greyish-green leaves turn a good colour in the autumn, the flowers having appeared in July, a good deal earlier than the evergreen kind and lasting well into September.

These trees will grow in any good rich soil, the American one disliking limy conditions, and it also does better in a slightly shadier part of the garden.

In very mild areas a tender variety, *I. yunnanensis*, which has white flowers and more elongated leaves, but is otherwise rather like *I. ilicifolia*, would be worth trying. But in general their tolerance seems to be around Zone 6–7.

JUGLANS

Juglans, the walnut, consists of about 16 deciduous species, grown and much prized for their beautiful timber and delicious nuts. The characteristic wood is grained in light and dark shades of a warm honey-brown and greatly valued for

19 *Itea ilicifolia*: Sweetspire

the making of furniture, especially veneers. The deeply fissured nut is one of the most popular in culinary use with its rich oily flavour.

The walnuts are mostly fast-growing trees, liking a good loamy soil, and should be sited in full sun with some protection from late frosts, which can damage the embryo foliage, and prevent the production of a good supply of nuts, which, anyway, don't appear till the trees are at least 10 years old.

Walnut leaves are pinnate and large, so they make excellent shade trees. In the case of *J. ailantifolia* from Japan, the leaves are over 3 ft (1 m) long on this slender upright species. The trunk is a pale grey with vertical fissures. The flowers are of separate sexes on the same tree, the male, graceful hanging greenish catkins, the female, in stalkless groups of 2–3, which become the large round green fruits 1½–2 in (4–5 cm) across. These blacken as they age and the two halves of the crinkly nut lie inside the casing.

J. regia, the Common Walnut, also known as the Persian or English Walnut, is one of the slower-growing species from Zone 5–6, and found in Europe, Asia and China and does not often reach above 50 ft (15 m). This tree gives the most delicious nuts and the finest timber of all, and the crushed leaves are fragrant. Though they are self-fruiting, if two varieties are planted together, the crop is more plentiful. The best form is *J. regia* 'Laciniata', the Cut-leaved Walnut, with much-divided leaves from drooping branches.

J. nigra, the Black Walnut, is from Central and Eastern America, South-east Canada and Zone 4, but is also grown in Europe. It reaches a great height, between 80 and 100 ft (25–30 m), and is much prized for its timber, though it is not so fine-grained as the English. The flowers come in early June, a little earlier than those of *J. regia*, and are hairy. But the resultant nuts are not so good as those of *J. regia*, being woody and small. The trunk can be enormous, as much as 20 ft (6 m) in circumference, a very dark brown, criss-crossed with lines of narrow ridges, whereas *J. regia*'s is grey and smooth with wide, deep ridges on ageing.

J. cinerea, the White Walnut or Butternut, is a fast grower and a native of Eastern North America and Zone 3, but does not grow so tall, around 50–60 ft (15–18 m), with a broad head, but not always symmetrical. The leaves are large, of 7–19 leaflets, and have a thick down on them. The fruits are larger, as much as 2½ in (6 cm) long, pointed at one end and sticky, as are the young shoots. The nuts are very oily and only favoured for pickling, or they are, sometimes, eaten fresh by the native Indians. The timber is not so highly prized, but *J. cinerea* makes one of the best shade trees.

Propagate by grafting, which produces better nuts than from seed. Plant in its permanent situation when young, as walnuts transplant badly after they are three years old. They must be pruned in full leaf in summer, or in autumn, never in winter or spring. A friend of mine learned this the hard way because when she cut some branches in winter the stumps wept and wept! When she pruned in summer's full leaf these leaves took up all the sap. Luckily the tree survived her mistake and she benefited from the lesson — gardening the tough way, but the best.

Walnuts have roots that produce a substance called juglone which is poisonous to surrounding shrubs and trees. It is particularly injurious to fruit

20 *Juglans ailantifolia*: Japanese Walnut

trees, and plants like tomatoes wont't grow under them. But I have found that other shrubs and plants grow quite happily under my old tree, although some species are more damaging than others, especially the American walnuts.

KOELREUTERIA

The Chinese Willow Pattern Tree, *Koelreuteria paniculata*, known also as Pride of India, China-tree and Goldenrain-tree, needs a hot dry summer to do well. It is hardy to Zone 5 except for prolonged and intense frost and likes a dry spot in the garden, out of the wind if possible, planted in rich soil so it will produce its erect sprays of yellow flowers, 6–12 in (15–30 cm) high, in July and August. The following bladder-like fruits gradually turn pink and remain on the tree all winter. The foliage, which begins with a reddish tinge, becomes a soft yellow before falling. It does not make a large tree in England, barely more than 20–30 ft (6–10 m), and *K. paniculata* 'Fastigiata' is even better for a small garden being slow-growing and forming a delightfully graceful column. There is a second species, *K. apiculata*, very similar but the pinnate leaves are double at the base, and it blooms sooner when young, which makes it the best one to plant when you want quick results.

One of the finest specimens of this tree in England can be seen at The Chelsea Physic Garden in London, growing in the unusually mild micro-climate bordering the river Thames.

LABURNUM

The laburnum is from a genus of only three species, all deciduous and native to Southern and Central Europe and easy as to soil, even good on dry shallow chalk. It has the rather romantic names of Golden Chain and Golden Rain Tree and certainly one in full flower can be a magnificent sight. I have the benefit of being able to see and enjoy the blaze of yellow when my neighbour's tree blooms, for all parts of the laburnum are poisonous, the seeds particularly, so it is not a tree to plant in the garden where young children may be playing. I do grow the evergreen form *Piptanthus nepalensis (laburnifolius)* but this is more shrub than tree-size and so I can quite easily remove the seed pods when they form.

The Common Laburnum is *L. anagyroides* which blooms in May with its hanging racemes of bright yellow pea flowers. A few weeks later the larger-growing Scotch Laburnum, *L. alpinum*, blooms with its smaller but more scented flowers in longer tresses and shiny sprays of leaves instead of the neater matt ones of the common variety. But the cross between these two, *L × wateri* 'Vossii', has produced the answer, beautiful chrome-yellow sprays 1½ ft (45 cm) long in June covering a tree with glossy leaves; being often sterile, it sets few of the poisonous seeds, and grows the fastest of the three, reaching around 30 ft (10 m) in 20 years. But of course it can be shaped and trained to a more modest size, if required, by spur pruning, and they can be grown as standards very effectively.

The laburnum is a very hardy tree to Zone 5 and will thrive in sun or shade.

With the heavy bunches of flowers, obviously it is better planted in a site protected from strong winds. As free-standing trees on a lawn they are one of the most floriferous of trees to have and make a stunning tunnel or pleached walk. There is a fine example of a tunnel, composed of the 'Vossii' cross, which makes an unbelievable cloud of yellow at Bodnant Gardens in North Wales. The bark of these trees is also very attractive, being shiny and smooth and of a browny-green colour.

LAGERSTROEMIA

Most of the species of lagerstroemia grow in tropical climates, but *L. indica* known as the Crape Myrtle will tolerate the conditions of a temperate climate and in southern parts of the British Isles, if given wall protection and a warm hot summer, will produce its flowers. It only makes a small tree and though deciduous it will not stand severe frosts. Consequently it is happiest in Southern Europe and warm areas of America like California, where it will reach 30 ft (10 m). It is native to China and is a wonderful sight when in full flower, the pale magenta panicles of curly petals are set against the leathery glaucous leaves.

I was quite stunned the first time I saw a lagerstroemia growing in a park in Hyères in the South of France. The blooms are so unusual, and their rich colour darkens as the day progresses. The bark of this very floriferous tree is smooth and a warm rose-mahogany colour. Altogether a tree worth trying to grow if you can find a protected corner in your garden, or have the good fortune to live in a climate with no appreciable frost.

LAURUS

Laurus nobilis, the Sweet Bay, Bay Laurel or Royal Bay, is a native of the Mediterranean area and can be seen growing wild there. But it will withstand quite low temperatures, to Zone 5, and there is always room for a bay tree in your garden. They make very handsome plants trained as a miniature tree in a tub or planted formally as a dividing row between one section of the garden and another. If the area is exposed to cold winds they will appreciate being placed against a fence for extra protection. Certainly the aromatic leaves do get browned by the wind, but in my garden I have two bay trees planted formally either side of a small wooden potting shed, where it is quite windy, but they have survived. If left to themselves they grow 20 ft (6 m) high, completely concealing the shed, but because of the occasional scorching and damage to the leaves which causes die-back and an untidy appearance, I wait till the more protected branches have flowered in the spring and then prune it well back, and it shoots out and very soon becomes totally green again. But I am always in a quandary when I leave them to grow tall and these two huge trees form a mass some 10 ft (3 m) around and make a grand sight overall but browned and dead-woody in patches. Should I trim them to neat small conical trees again, like sentinels either side of the potting shed door, or leave the amorphous mass to make a bold pattern in the garden? I think the answer is to have the pleasure of both, and leave the large trees unpruned for a few years and then, when one is

8 *Cercis siliquastrum* 'Rubra': Red Judas Tree

9 *Davidia involucrata*: Handkerchief Tree

in a strong-willed frame of mind, take the saw and secateurs and carve them into a more manageable shape.

The female trees have shiny black fruits after the scented greeny-yellow flowers, and there are two varieties, *L. nobilis angustifolia*, the Willow-leaf Bay, with slimmer leaves, less shiny and paler, but this is a hardier form. *L. nobilis* 'Aurea' has butter-yellow leaves which I do not think make such a good contrast against the fluffy bunches of flowers in April.

Bay is easy as to soil, as long as it is well-drained, and it tolerates salty winds from the sea better than intense frosts further inland, which may be the reason why my trees have survived for over 30 years, despite being exposed to the full force of westerly gales from the shore half a mile (0.8 km) away.

The thick leathery leaves, deliciously spicy when crushed, are used for cooking and can be hung in bunches to dry and preserve. But they are a better flavour, naturally, taken straight from the tree and added to stews, soups, particularly anything having tomatoes as an ingredient. So keep a small bay tree in a pot on the kitchen window-sill. Long ago the leaves were used to flavour rice puddings. But always take care to remove them before serving the dish, as I once saw a person choke on a bay leaf — luckily not fatally, but very unpleasant and frightening.

LIGUSTRUM

Ligustrum, the Privet, is a member of the olive family and consists of about 50 species of mostly evergreen shrubs and trees. These are usually grown and clipped hard so the flowers don't get much of a chance to remain on the bush, and this is a pity as they can be very decorative. But one or two of the privet species will grow into beautifully ornamental trees and they can be useful in many situations as they relish poor dry soils and grow very fast, though they do take a lot from the surrounding soil, to the detriment of neighbouring plants. They will tolerate some shade but are basically sun-loving.

The Glossy or Tree Privet or Woa Tree from China and Zone 7, *L. lucidum*, makes the finest tree, growing to about 50 ft (15 m), with a dark grey bark, streaked a lighter shade. The small fragrant creamy-white bisexual flowers in 5–8 in (12–20 cm) sprays open in early September, at a time when not many other trees are flowering, followed by ½ in (1.2 cm) long black oval berries, with an attractive bluish bloom. Some people find the scent of the flowers rather overpoweringly sweet, but I like it. The leaves are slim, long, and pointed and a rich dark green, extremely shiny above with a reddish tinge when young. It forms a dense small evergreen tree, ideal as a specimen in a sheltered part of the garden, and in Southern Europe it is often used to line the boulevards.

There are three interesting forms: *L. lucidum* 'Excelsum Superbum' has variegated leaves which are edged chrome-yellow and buff-white and is a little less hardy than the type, so needs more careful siting to protect the young growths from cold winds; *L. lucidum* 'Latifolium' has very attractive leaves, as large as those of camellia; and *L. lucidum* 'Tricolor' has narrow leaves edged with white and touched with pink when young.

Another species from China that is deciduous and makes a very good flowering tree, being closely packed with dense sprays of clear-white flowers in July, is *L. sinense*. The leaves are oblong and tomentose and the fruits are black with a purple tinge. There is a variegated form, *L. sinense* 'Variegatum', with mild greenish-grey and white leaves, and a charming minature, *L. sinense nanum*, which is almost evergreen, with a horizontal way of growing with dense spikes of creamy-white flowers, so thickly produced as to hide the leaves. A very desirable variety that would look extremely attractive grown in a large pot or tub.

Prune these tree privets only when necessary, by cutting any superfluous branches in spring. Propogate by taking hardwood cuttings in autumn and place them out of doors; or they can be done earlier, during the summer, and put in a cold frame.

LIQUIDAMBAR

Liquidambar, from the same family as the Witch Hazel, is a small genus of deciduous trees, three of which are cultivated, but the Sweet Gum or Red Gum, *L. styraciflua*, is the one must commonly grown. It is from the south-eastern United States and Zone 5 and makes a very large tree, growing to 150 ft (45 m) in the wild, but in cultivation about 20 ft (6 m) in 20 years, keeping a neat pyramidal shape, so is fine for the average garden. The leaves, at first glance, are like those of the maple but arranged alternately, whereas on the maple they are opposite each other. The Sweet Gum has 6 in (15 cm) wide five- or seven-lobed bright green leaves, finely toothed and glossy. On the undersides the vein axils have browny-orange tufts. The greenish-yellow flowers open in May on the same tree, the males a 2–3 in (5–8 in) long spike of round heads, and the females much smaller, barely ½ in (1.2 cm) and usually in pairs or singly. The woody fruits, hanging on long stalks, are round, 1–1½ in (2.5–4 cm) across, and covered with bristles. But the chief attraction of *L. styraciflua* is the beautiful autumn colours of its leaves which become brilliant red, orange, yellow and purple, particularly if grown in the moist soil near ponds or streams. The bark has deep fissures — even on the young branches — and other branchlets form corky wings. The timber of this attractive tree is known as Satin Walnut; and both the wood and the leaves are aromatic.

There are four forms with different coloured leaves. In *L. styraciflua* 'Aurea' they are mottled and striped yellow; in *L. styraciflua* 'Variegata' the leaves are edged with white, and have pink tints in autumn; *L. styraciflua* 'Lane Roberts', a particularly choice one, has autumn colour of an incredibly dark blackish-crimson; and *L. styraciflua* 'Golden Treasure' has leaves with chrome-yellow margins.

The Oriental Sweet Gum from Asia Minor and Zone 6, *L. orientalis*, will make a modest specimen in Britain and is, anyway, a slow-growing tree with much smaller hairless leaves. In its native conditions it will grow to 100 ft (30 m) but with our climate it makes quite a suitable size for garden planting. Unfortunately, its leaves do not become quite so gloriously coloured in autumn.

The Chinese Sweet Gum, *L. formosana* from Taiwan and southern China, is a smaller tree from Zone 7, but is, nevertheless, quite hardy given good protection from the worst of the winter and the late frosts in spring. The leaves are 3–5-lobed, hairy underneath, and a soft green with purple tints in spring and again in autumn. A form from China discovered by E.H. Wilson, *L. formosana monticola*, seems much hardier, the leaves being very large, 3-lobed, and hairless, with the same attractive spring and autumn colours, though not so harsh as those of *L. styraciflua*.

Propagation can be from seed, but it takes a long time to germinate, so layering in spring is more satisfactory. Liquidambars need a lime-free soil, moist and well-drained and a sunny position or light shade; they do not like dry chalky ground. Any pruning or shaping of young trees should be done in winter, while the trees are dormant.

LIRIODENDRON

The Tulip Tree or Yellow Poplar, *Liriodendron*, is very hardy, even in Zone 4, and easy as to soil. It has very beautiful leaves shaped wider than longer, as the end looks cut off leaving two other pointed lobes on each side of the spine. They turn a soft and pleasant yellow in autumn before falling. Unfortunately, the flowers take a long time to appear. I planted a tree in my garden because I saw a beautiful specimen in another garden long ago, and mine has now passed the 23 years I understood it needed for it to flower. Recently I was told it must be 30 ft (10 m) high before it produces, which it has not quite reached. The blooms are rather like tulips in shape, greenish-white with an orange mark at the centre, and appearing in June or July.

The species most often planted is *L. tulipifera* from North America, but there is a rarer form from China, *L. chinense*, with smaller green flowers, yellow inside, but this does not bloom so freely which is a disadvantage.

But I think the best form for a medium-sized garden is *L. tulipifera* 'Fastigiatum' which grows fairly quickly into a slender, columnar shape, so not only does it take up little space and light, but it can add a graceful pencil form to the other shapes in the garden.

MAGNOLIA

There are about 80 species of magnolia, most of them deciduous but several choice evergreens. One of the smallest and most delightful magnolias to grow in any size garden is *M. stellata*. It produces its glistening white flowers on bare branches at an early age and rarely grows more than 10 ft (3 m) high. There is a pink variety in two shades, *M. stellata* 'Rosea' or 'Rubra', but the best is perhaps *M. stellata* 'Water Lily' with its larger flowers; and a cross between *M. stellata* and *M. kobus* has given a very early-flowering and desirable variety, *M. × loebneri* 'Leonard Messel'. This has the useful property of doing well in a chalky soil and is also hardy.

I have a heavy clay soil so I cannot grow a very choice magnolia, the lime-hating *M. sieboldii*, but I have recently given a plant to my sister and it has settled down well in her acid soil, and I hope one day to see the fragrant pure-white flowers which, at the centre of the cup-shaped blooms, have such showy and distinctive crimson stamens. There is a fairly young tree in Sissinghurst Castle Gardens in Kent, where the original one was killed by a recent severe winter. The unusual blooms appear from late April and throughout the summer.

The finest deciduous specimen, again not tolerant of lime, is *M. campbellii*, the Pink Tulip Tree. The hybrid *M. campbellii* 'Charles Raffill' has the benefit of an early-flowering habit (about 12 years) of one of its crosses *M. mollicomata* because the true type *M. campbellii* does not flower till it is 20–30 years old, too long for most of us to wait. But it is worth hunting out fine examples of this tree in other gardens, to see it flowering in February. There is a magnificent 50 ft (15 m) tree in Overbecks Garden at Salcombe in Devon growing against terraced walls so that you can lean over high up and the flowers can be seen at really close quarters. Even in the South of England the enormous blooms, which open goblet-shaped, pink or white, and splay out to reach 10 in (25 cm) across, will be damaged by frost and so must be protected from it, or else grown in a virtually frost-free climate and zone.

The finest evergreen is perhaps *M. grandiflora* with its huge leathery leaves and scented white flowers in late summer, which can reach 10 in (25 cm) across and one flower makes a stunning centrepiece for the dining-table. Unless in a very protected garden, this magnolia is usually grown against the south wall of a house in England, but in Southern France or the south-eastern United States, where the temperature is normally at least ten degrees warmer, there are wonderful groups of these trees, free-standing, in gardens and parks. They can grow eventually to 100 ft (30 m) high, reaching 20 ft (6 m) in 20 years, and are clothed in their glossy evergreen leaves, a reddish down underneath, among which the creamy flowers can be seen blooming in the summer sunshine. And there have recently been reports of a fine tree believed to be growing in a now wild site of an old convent garden in Portugal. It is reputed to be 200 years old and about 80–90 ft (25–27 m) high.

The four modest magnolia trees I am growing in my garden are all around 10 ft (3 m) high so far. I have a young *M. grandiflora* 'Exmouth', the variety which is said to flower early and has been planted on the south wall of the house. It gets rather blasted by westerly gales, so I have planted an escallonia bush either side to form an evergreen protective screen, which has saved its great leaves from getting battered so much in the wind, and I hope will protect the flowers, too, when they come. As the escallonia, with its glossy sticky leaves, likes sea air and has good pink flowers, it has made quite a nice arrangement and frame for the magnolia. Then I have a *M. stellata* which has good furry buds to protect the unopened flowers during winter and a fence behind it to save the starry blooms, when they open, from getting damaged. My fig tree has rather overgrown itself and hangs above my *M. × soulangiana* 'Lennei', but it does give it protection when the goblet-shaped flowers bloom in April — pale rose, touched with white and purple.

The fourth tree I planted at the top of the rockery and it dominates the whole area when it flowers with its slim purple tulip-shaped blooms. This is *M. liliiflora* 'Nigra' and is in flower for many weeks from April onwards. But the habit of this and of *M. stellata* is rather branched and shrubby, though I imagine they could be trained into a tree shape, on a single trunk, if the lower branches were removed.

MALUS

This genus was formerly included with *Pyrus* (Pear) and is composed of some 35 species of tree with a large number of cultivars. They are all very free-flowering in spring and many have showy fruits in autumn (see Chapter 2 for some species with edible fruits). *Malus*, the botanical name of both Apples and Crabs, is the original Roman name of the wild European species. This *M. sylvestris* has white flowers and is rather thorny, so is not often seen in cultivation, though it still grows in Europe and Asia Minor and can be as much as 45 ft (13 m) high.

The japanese Crab, *M. floribunda*, is a graceful small tree with arching branches of rose pink then white flowers, which are carmine when in bud, all three colours being displayed together. It is an ideal size for the small garden and one of the earliest to flower, any time from April to June, and growing 20–30 ft (6–9 m). The slim glossy leaves are toothed and can occasionally be lobed. The tiny round fruits ripen yellow and red in October.

M. halliana from China and Zone 5 is an attractive small tree to 15 ft (5 m) with narrow, glossy, dark green leaves, a good contrast for the shell pink flowers which are rosy-red in bud. The fruits are only pea-sized and of little ornamental value.

M. ioensis, the Iowa Crab or Prairie Crab is very hardy and from Zone 2 and has the largest flowers of any crab. There is a semi-double variety called *M. ioensis* 'Plena', Bechtel's Crab, with 2–2½ in (5–6 cm) soft pink blooms in clusters of 4–6 and delicately fragrant. It flowers quite late in June and needs a good, rich loamy soil to give of its best and does not like chalk.

M. ioensis is similar to the Sweet Crab Apple, *M. coronaria*, but the round greenish-yellow fruits have a duller surface and the branches and underneath of the leaves are more downy. It grows 30 ft (9 m) in the wild, but is often quite dwarfed in cultivation, so a very desirable tree for decorating the garden.

M. hupehensis is from China and Zone 4 with upright branches and it grows taller than some of the crabs and can reach 40 ft (12 m), though normally around 25 ft (8 m). The long slim leaves, and the single white fragrant flowers in May and June, are followed by small fruit on long stalks, which ripen from orange and yellow to red in September, making a very alluring tree. When mature the brownish-grey bark flakes attractively. The leaves were once used in China for making tea.

M. × purpurea 'Eleyi' of Zone 4 is known as the Purple Crab and has deep purple flowers and matching bronzy leaves and rich purple conical fruits in autumn, growing to around 25 ft (8 m). Two other good hybrids with similar colouring are *M. × purpurea* 'Profusion', and *M. × purpurea* 'Pendula' — also known as 'Echtermeyer' — which is a delightful weeping tree, low and wide-spreading.

Malus 'Magdeburgensis' is a lovely little broad-headed tree for a small corner, with large semi-double flowers in April and May, which are crimson in bud and open to a pale purple touched with white, the fruits that follow are yellowish-green. This is a fascinating hybrid between *M. spectabilis*, the Chinese Crab, and *M. pumila*, the French Paradise Apple.

Malus 'Van Eseltine' of Zone 4 is an excellent tree to grow where space is very restricted, for although it can reach 20 ft (6 m), it adopts a conical shape, with semi-double flowers 2 in (5 cm) across in solid clusters, which open to pale pink in May; in early autumn there are yellow and red fruits.

Malus 'Red Jade', also of Zone 4 and growing to about the same height, makes an elegant weeping tree with bright green young foliage and pink and white flowers in spring. Cherry-sized crimson fruits hang on the bare branches far into winter, so that it is attractive at any time, though it tends to fruit every other year. Prune any ground suckers to keep a good shape. This tree originated at the Brooklyn Botanic Garden.

M. tschonoskii makes an erect pyramidal tree up to 40 ft (12 m) with broadly ovate and pointed leaves, irregularly incised. The rose-tinted buds open white in May, followed by greenish-yellow fruits, touched with purple. But the main feature of this species is the beautiful autumn colouring of the leathery leaves, which turn orange, yellow, red and purple. Again a useful tree for a confined space or a very narrow garden, and often used for lining streets, though not quite so hardy, to Zone 5, as some of the other species.

The Flowering Crabs are all very easy to grow, tolerating any kind of soil, though appreciating a good helping of peat and compost when being planted.

When propagating, the species can be grown from seed, but the hybrids are usually grafted on apple stocks, to give standards or half-standards, as required.

Prune to form round heads, and cut back and thin any rampant growths after flowering.

MYRTUS

The myrtles are very old and attractive plants to grow — famous in antiquity — and *M. communis* is the one species that is found all over Europe, from a large tropical family, in a genus of 100 shrubs and trees. Though it prefers mild conditions, I have found it will survive with me and has done so through very cold winters, particularly the so-called dwarf variety *M. communis tarentina*. This plant was so happy in the warm spot I had found for it near a wall and growing through gravel — which gave it additional reflected heat whenever the sun was shining — that it eventually became a large bush or small tree. The tiny evergreen, attractively glossy leaves are aromatic when crushed and the flowers, coming from buds like round red balls, open to a bunch of sweetly scented creamy flowers, followed by white fruits with the miniature *M. communis tarentina* and black fruits with the common one, *M. communis*.

The larger *M. apiculata* from Chile will grow to 25 ft (8 m) in a favoured location, whereas the previous plants are not likely to reach more than 10 ft (3 m). In a sheltered site it is a lovely tree to have in the garden for the rich tan bark adds to the variety of colour of other nearby trees as it gradually peels off to reveal a soft and smooth creamy texture underneath. *M. apiculata* leaves are ovate and a matt green, the undersides being a shade paler. The white blooms are produced individually, not in opposite pairs as in *M. communis*, and the berries that follow are both black and red and sweet enough to eat. *M. communis* flowers in July and August, and *M. apiculata* a little later, from August onwards; and they remain in flower well into October.

Another desirable myrtle, tender like *M. apiculata*, is *M. lechlerana*, also from Chile. Its tall thin trunks look like giant cinnamon sticks, strangely powdery. The sweet-scented flowers come in May, followed by edible black and red berries. The leaves are small and ovate, on red stalks, first bronzy, then turning a rich shiny green.

Myrtles are not fussy as to soil, and will tolerate lime and chalk. They are particularly happy near the sea, standing up very well to any salty winds. Like the arbutus trees they seem to find the climate of southern Ireland very agreeable and grow there prolifically. The best time to propagate these myrtles is in July or August, by taking cuttings of half-ripened wood. They are well worth trying, for if you plant in a good sheltered site — ideally they like to be in Zone 6, through to Zone 8 in the case of *M. apiculata* — it is exciting to find they do thrive and can grow to the size of a small tree. They would be perfect in a small walled garden, as long as they have well-drained soil and a sunny position. The scent of the whole plant is alluring, for the fruit and flowers, as well as the leaves, are rich in aromatic oil known as 'Eau d'Anges' and used when making perfumes.

NOTHOFAGUS

The Nothofagus or Southern Beech comprise a small genus of trees, several of which are being tried out in plantings in a Scottish glen and elsewhere, in order to find a suitable replacement for the lost elms; for they grow exceedingly fast. But they are not as resistant to wind as the elms are; nevertheless, they will grow quickly in a rich well-drained soil, as long as it is not chalky and the site itself is well protected from gales. They herald from the southern hemisphere and are deciduous as well as evergreen. They are related to the beeches of the northern hemisphere but have much smaller leaves, though the same distinctive three-cornered nuts.

One of the fastest growers is *N. procera* from Chile, with shiny toothed indented leaves, sometimes 4 in (10 cm) long, which turn to a vivid colour of red and yellow. *N. obliqua*, the Roblé Beech, also from Chile, but not growing so tall and also deciduous, quickly makes a lovely columnar shape with its similarly large leaves. An evergreen which develops an elegant pyramidal shape is *N. betuloides*, but this is a more tender species and better grown in areas like the South-West of England, where the smaller glossy green leaves will mass densely on the branches, making a most attractive tree.

But perhaps the best tree for the smaller garden is the deciduous Antarctic Beech, *N. antarctica*. The trunk and leading stems often take on an interesting twisting effect, and in a nice sunny site, which these trees do require, it makes a very excellent contribution to a garden picture. In late spring little clumps of yellow flowers are grouped along the branches among the leaves. The variety *N.*

antarctica 'Benmore', which is prostrate in form, makes a dense round shape of interweaving branches covered with the small shiny heart-shaped leaves and producing good and varied autumn colour.

NYSSA

The Nyssa, Black Gum or Sour Gum is a very small genus of trees which are planted for their brilliant autumn colour, their flowers and fruits being small and inconspicuous. It is of the same family, *Davidiaceae*, as the Handkerchief Tree and is to be seen at its best in eastern North America, where it colours wonderfully, and grows to much greater heights (100 ft, 30 m) than in England, where it does well in the south, growing at first conical and spreading with age to a broadly columnar outline and up to 30 ft (10 m). It is very hardy, tolerating Zone 4, and happy in sun or semi-shade in not too exposed a position.

There is a spectacular display to be seen at Sheffield Park in Sussex, some of them in the moist soil they prefer, surrounding water, and where the brilliance of their leaves as they turn from rich glossy green to gold, and in a good season to a flaming red, is dramatically mirrored in the rippling water.

N. sylvatica, the Tupelo or Pepperidge, is slow-growing and needs to be planted very young as it is not happy when its roots are disturbed if it is moved when it has attained some size. So plant from a container into lime-free soil with as little disturbance as possible. The oval or obovate leaves, which can be up to 6 in (15 cm) long, are untoothed, tapered at both ends and usually shiny, but sometimes a matt green on the surface. There is an excellent variety named *N. sylvatica* 'Sheffield Park' which colours several weeks before the common one, so providing a longer period of wonderful hues overall. Therefore, if you are keen to have some of the finest autumn colour in your garden, this is the tree to plant.

Propogate by seed under glass in autumn, but raised from seed it does show great variations.

OSTRYA

The Ostrya makes up a small genus of deciduous trees related to the hornbeams, and with similar foliage, three types of which are usually cultivated. The Hop Hornbeam, *O. carpinifolia* from southern Europe, but hardy in Zone 5, is so-called because after attractive yellow catkins in spring, the 2 in (5 cm) long fruits which follow have seeds within a bladder-type greenish-white husk and look like those of the hop. It is the male catkins that are so conspicuous hanging down as long as 3 in (8 cm), the female being small, upright at first and gradually turning downwards.

The American *O. virginiana* has the very hard wood typical of this genus, and is known as Ironwood, and grows into a smaller, neat and nicely shaped tree, the fruit-husks being golden-brown. The variety that usually makes the tallest specimen is from Japan, *O. japonica*, the Japanese Hop Hornbeam, with particularly downy soft leaves, and green fruits.

All these trees are easy to grow in a good, well-drained soil, the American variety preferring a sunny position, and making a wonderful sight in autumn when the characteristically toothed leaves turn an eye-catching golden-yellow overall.

The foliage of *O. carpinifolia* turns a lighter, sharper yellow; but though difficult to find in England, the *O. virginiana* would be the one I would choose to grow as it rarely reaches more than 40 ft (12 m) when fully mature, hardly two-thirds the eventual height of the other varieties.

OXYDENDRUM

Oxydendrum arboreum (occasionally *Oxydendron*) is a genus having only one species, belonging to the heath family, of which it is the tallest deciduous member. This tree is also known as *Andromeda arborea* or, commonly, the Sorrel or Sourwood Tree.

At first glance it could be mistaken for an enormous pieris, with its similar sprays of waxy-white flowers, like those of the lily of the valley. They hang in 10 in (25 cm) clusters from the tips of the shoots in July, remaining on the tree till September. Then the smooth rich green tapered leaves, about 5 in (12 cm) long with a faintly bronze tint, turn brilliant colours of yellow, orange, scarlet and purple, making it an outstanding specimen for autumn colour alone.

In eastern North America it will grow to 60 ft (18 m) in the wild, but in cultivation it rarely reaches more than 20 ft (6 m) and sometimes much less; and with branches right to the ground it can appear quite shrubby at this height.

It is best grown in semi-shade — though it is also happy in full sun — in moist, rich neutral to acid soil, never dry or limy, and within the shelter of neighbouring trees; a similar situation to that enjoyed by eucryphias and rhododendrons. It is hardy to Zone 5.

The flowers are sweetly scented and very attractive to bees. The leaves have an acid taste like sorrel and are not unpleasant when chewed, in fact, they were used in pharmacy, as a diuretic or tonic. The fruits are tough, hairy, bell-like capsules.

Oxydendrum is easily raised from seed in February, but also by layering, or from cuttings. The general shape of the tree is very elegant, tall and slim, with the horizontal branches drooping towards their ends, so that the flower racemes give a graceful but solid, rounded effect.

PARROTIA

Parrotia persica, the Iron Tree or Persian Witch Hazel from North Iran and the Caucasus and Zone 5, makes a small tree, never growing more than 25–30 ft (8–10 m) high, and although a member of the hamamelis family, it is very tolerant of lime in the soil, also liking it moist, but well-drained, to produce its best results. I grow mine splayed against a tall brick wall of the house because they like to spread out horizontally, but can be grown free-standing in the border if carefully trained upright when young.

One of the features of this tree is the gorgeous colour change of the 3–4 in

(8–10 cm) long toothed leaves, from bright green all summer, then gradually becoming gold and crimson towards winter.

There is an effective weeping form *P. persica* 'Pendula', which becomes a dome of bright colour, eventually 10 ft (3 m) overall. The flowers are unusual, being strung along the branches in early spring. Small red clusters of stamens within rich-brown bracts appear from woolly buds. Another feature is that the bark of older branches and the main trunk becomes attractively grey and peeling — said to be reminiscent of the London Plane.

PAULOWNIA

Visitors leaving the railway station a few miles from my home are usually looking straight ahead of them to catch a glimpse of the sea. But if they should happen to glance to their left, above them on the incline which leads over the hill to the main part of the town, there stands an old and gnarled paulownia tree, the Mountain Jacaranda. It is now on a derelict piece of land but at one time there was a nursery on the site and before that, years ago, the land belonged to a member of the Royal Horticultural Society. It may have been this person who planted this tree at the beginning of the century. It has braved all the storms, winds and wartime bombs thrown at it and still survives. The only hazard it really has to surmount is the protection of its flower-buds, which form in autumn and remain on the tree through the winter, to flower in late spring if not badly damaged by frost. The blooms are upright clusters of heliotrope, the individual trumpets like foxgloves, marked with a darker purple and touched with yellow at their base.

The one that flowers earliest is *P. fargesii* but it grows quite tall and there are several other species. *P. tomentosa* (*imperialis*) has darker flowers but is not quite so hardy, though being more compact in growth it is easier to site in a protected place in the garden. The leaves of this tree are also spectacular, being heart-shaped and of enormous size, sometimes nearly 1 ft (30 cm) long and a rich green with a downy underside. These can be encouraged to become even larger if the tree is pruned to the ground in spring and the resultant rapid growth can produce a leader of some 6–10 ft (2–3 m) draped with quite huge, but elegant leaves. And this will make an attractive dome of green if you should want quick results in a small space, even in a tub, though, of course, it will not have the lovely scented flowers, or look like a proper tree. This will take about 25 years to reach maturity, but during this time your paulownia will give a great deal of pleasure as it grows and what excitement when it eventually flowers for you.

They were introduced to France first from Japan, but originally came from China. There are very fine specimens of the longest cultivated species *P. tomentosa* still to be seen gracing the beautiful Jardin des Plantes in Paris.

PICRASMA

Picrasma quassioides is related to *Ailanthus* but never reaching more than two-thirds of its height — around 40 ft (12 m). It is a completely hardy (Zone 4)

21 *Paulownia tomentosa*

deciduous species of a genus of mostly tropical trees found in China, Korea and the Himalayas, and is a particular feature in Japan, where it gives the most dramatic orange and crimson colour in autumn. It is not quite so flamboyant in England and is not a very common tree anyway, but it has very graceful pinnate leaves 6–12 in (15–30 cm) long, composed of up to 13 leaflets. The sprays of tiny green flowers open in June and by October the ball-like fruits that have formed have turned scarlet, makling it very decorative.

Plant it in any soil; it will grow in lime but does better in a neutral or even acid one. Choose a well-drained site in sun or half-shade. I think it is always interesting to have an unusual tree in the garden to mix among the very well-known and often-planted species. The bark of picrasma is exceptionally bitter, as, indeed, is the rest of this tree, but it is so attractive, particularly if you like bright autumn colour.

PLATANUS

The Plane Tree, *Platanus*, consists of a genus of about ten deciduous species, generally of the northern hemisphere. It is often used for planting in cities because it will tolerate most conditions, but prefers well-drained soil and a sunny site. It is just as happy in rural surroundings, and a specimen tree standing in isolation in the countryside is a noble sight with its alternately leaved maple-like foliage, though what distinguishes it are the spiky fruit-balls which hang from the strangely crooked branches in strings of two to six, and in winter make a fascinating tracery against the sky.

The famous so-called London Plane, *P.* × *hispanica*, makes a magnificent tree, growing quickly to around 30 ft (10 m) in 15–20 years. This tree, with its tall bare trunk, is to be seen all over Central and Western Europe, in parks and gardens and lining many a city street. It is generally believed to be a cross between *P. orientalis* and *P. occidentalis*. The grey-green bark has a mottled look, flaking to reveal smooth lighter creamy patches; this wood makes an excellent veneer being very finely grained. Tolerant of Zone 5, the large 3–5-lobed, often variable, dark green shiny palmate leaves are very decorative, turning orange and yellow in autumn. The flowers are very small, opening in May, with separate sexes on the same tree, the reddish females clustered at the tip of the shoots and the smaller males, yellow, grouped further back on the old wood. But the fruit-balls remain effectively on the tree all winter, turning brown in autumn and eventually breaking up to reveal hairy nutlets in spring. An attractive form *P.* × *hispanica* 'Suttneri', has leaves where the green is marked with creamy streaks, and touched with pink when young, becoming dark green, so giving a pretty, variegated effect. It was said that the plane, when well grown and rooted, 'has never been known to blow down'. It was certainly put to the test and found wanting during the night of the hurricane (or, strictly speaking, the vortex) in South-East England in October 1987!

P. occidentalis the Buttonwood or American Sycamore, from Zone 4, grows to even greater heights, as much as 150 ft (45 m) in the eastern part of the United States and south Ontario, but is not quite so easy to grow in England, as it is susceptible to the frosts we get in spring. The leaves are up to 9 in (23 cm) across and have shallower lobes, and the fruits are single and smooth. The bark, when new, is creamy-white, becoming a pattern of buff and green.

P. orientalis is from South-East Europe and known as the Oriental Plane or Chennar Tree. With its stout short trunk and elegant spreading, but rounded, head of branches giving good shade, this tree is very long-lived, even in England. W.J. Bean, once Curator at the Royal Botanic Gardens at Kew, mentions that there are believed to be still trees on the banks of the Bosphorus which were there in the days of the Crusades in 1069. It is able to tolerate hot summers and very cold winters — though from Zone 6 — and will also grow on chalky dry soil, where the other planes will not do so well. But in the heat of Southern Europe, *P. orientalis* is often planted in the moister soil near water. The toothed 5-lobed leaves, up to 9 in (23 cm) wide, are so deeply cut they are almost divided to the stalk, and turn a lovely soft bronze in autumn. The fruits are bristly like the London Plane but with 3–6 on one stalk instead of 2–4. The bark flakes but has a rougher surface.

Though not for the average garden, these planes can be lopped or pollarded to keep them to a more manageable size, and trained well when young. But there is a variety of the Oriental Plane, *P. orientalis insularis*, the Cyprian Plane, which makes a very much smaller tree and has smaller even more deeply cut leaves, and grows to a very charming shape, with its delicate light green foliage. So this would be the one to plant where space is restricted.

Propagation is by layering, or by cuttings, in late summer, as it rarely comes well from seed.

POPULUS

The Poplar Tree, *Populus*, is a genus of about 35 deciduous species, most of them totally unsuitable for the average garden, not only because they grow tall very quickly but their roots extend great distances and cause disruption to houses and walls. But as a screen at the bottom of a fairly large garden they make a good wind-break, particularly near the coast. They like any moist soils, except chalk, and prefer wet areas, as on the banks of rivers.

The White Poplar or Abele, *P. alba*, is tolerant of Zone 3 and naturalised in Britain, but originally from West Asia, West Siberia and South and Central Europe. It has white undersides to the leaves, which gives the tree an attractive green and white effect, especially in a breeze. When first open, the lobed leaves are completely covered in the thick white down, then the upper sides become green and glossy, turning yellow in autumn in Europe, but red in America. The lead grows very fast and if it is left 'feathered' with young growth down the stem for some time, this will delay the tendency to sucker. The form *P. alba* 'Richardii' would be the best of this species to plant as it grows far less quickly and to a much smaller size. The leaves are still white underneath but a lovely chrome-yellow above, giving a very pleasing appearance with its smooth, grey and white bark marked in diamond-shaped patterns. This poplar, unusually, will grow on chalk and in fairly dry conditions, unlike most of the other species.

When a poplar tree is mentioned, most people think of the tall slim columns of the Lombardy Poplar, *Populus* 'Italica', which line the roads of North

America and northern France (as does the Grey Poplar, *P.* × *canescens*). This form of *P. nigra*, the Black Poplar of Zone 2 (which can reach 130 ft), will only grow to 90 ft (27 m) but being so narrow with erect branches, *P. nigra* 'Italica' or 'Pyramidalis' could be planted well away from anything its roots might disrupt, and as it makes 2 ft (60 cm) a year it is a handsome tree to see, especially from a distance. It does well in full sun and in warm summers. The Lombardy Poplars are mostly male clones with 2 in (5 cm) long reddish catkins in March or April. The fluted grey bark produces twiggy shoots.

But not quite so tall is a variety of the Black Italian Poplar named *P.* 'Serotina Aurea', the Golden Poplar, especially if it is regularly pruned to keep a neat small shape. The leaves are bright yellow at first, showing a touch of green on them in summer and returning to pure yellow before they fall.

P. lasiocarpa, the Chinese Necklace Poplar from Central China and Zone 5, has even larger leaves, as much as 10 in (25 cm) long, and are a delightful sharp green, heart-shaped, attached to long red stalks. The young twigs are hairy, the upper part of the leaves becoming quite smooth. *P. lasiocarpa* has male and female flowers on the same tree which appear in late April or May, both about 4 in (10 cm) long, the males reddish and the females a greeny-yellow. The resultant fruiting catkins are sometimes 8 in (20 cm) long, a string of 20 little green fruits which disperse their cottony seeds in mid-summer. This tree is not so fast-growing — just over 1 ft (30 cm) a year — and the maximum height is 65 ft (19 m). It seems to do best in the south-western areas of Britain.

Of the many poplar species with their varying shapes and heights and style of catkins, there is a native of Europe, including Britain, Asia and North Africa, *P. tremula*, the Aspen, that is attractive in habit as the leaves are on long thin stalks which are flattened and cause them to tremble in the wind. They are almost circular with toothed wavy edges and grey-green and hairy, turning in late autumn to a soft smooth yellow. The greyish-pink male and female catkins appear in February, a cheerful sight in winter, before the leaves come, followed by the fruiting catkins in May when they shed their white woolly seeds. The bark is very smooth and grey with horizontal lines, and this tree often reaches only 35 ft (11 m).

There is a very elegant form, the Weeping Aspen, *P. tremula* 'Pendula', which becomes umbrella-shaped, with its branches hanging in February with greyish-mauve male catkins 2–4 in (5–10 cm) long. It can be grown successfully on a large lawn, where the regular grass-cutting will keep any suckers at bay. When grafted, it barely reaches a neat 8–10 ft (2.5–3 m) in height.

The American, False or Quaking Aspen, *P. tremuloides* from northern Mexico to Alaska, and south of the tundra in Canada, is able to tolerate Zone 1 and will grow as high above sea-level as 10,000 ft (3,050 m). It makes quite a small-sized tree in Britain, though to 100 ft (30 m) or so in the wild. The flowers, appearing in late February, are slimmer than *P. tremula* and when young the trunk and the branches are yellower and paler with dark horizontal markings; the leaves are smaller, finely-toothed, and even more delicately feathering to the wind. They are smooth, dark green with paler undersides, turning bright yellow in autumn. This species prefers a friable light soil. In Alaska it is known as The Popple. The weeping form, *P. tremuloides* 'Pendula', has the charming name of Parasol de St Julien, as it originated in France in 1865. It is a female tree and makes an elegant shape for the garden with its pendant branches.

If you have room for a big poplar and want a really fast-grower, *P.* 'Robusta' will reach 90 ft (27 m) in 20 years with a wonderfully straight trunk. It is a cross between *P. angulata* and *P. nigra* 'Plantierensis' with copper-coloured young leaves, becoming blue-green through the summer, and downy twigs; and like *P. nigra* 'Italica' it is a male clone.

An attractive variegated form of *P. × candicans*, the Ontario or Balm of Gilead Poplar, which is from Zone 4, always female and known as 'Aurora', has heart-shaped leaves which, on first opening, deliciously scent the air with balsam. The older leaves become green but are cream at first, touched with pink. This variety does well if the shoots are pruned back in early spring, so giving more of the lovely young colour.

Poplars, being so fast growing, can be used after 30 years for timber, but as the wood is very light and porous it is only serviceable for match-making (*P. tremula* and *P. × canadensis*) and articles like packing cases — for it has no smell — and planking (*P. alba*).

The poplars are usually propagated from cuttings, which take easily. Some can be grown from seed but the male clones, of course, must be cutting-propagated. Prune always in summer, not in spring or winter.

PRUNUS

There is an enormous range of trees in the genus of the prunus, most of them grown for their spectacular blossom and beautiful leaf colour. Those that produce fruit large enough to eat are described in the chapter on Fruiting Trees (Chapter 2) and the ones I mention here are purely ornamental.

This ornamental group of the prunus, popularly known as the Flowering Cherries, produces blooms with single or double, white or pale to deep pink flowers; and they either have green leaves, some of which turn in autumn, or they are purple-leaved from the outset, providing a rich copper foliage against the delicately coloured blooms.

There are four main divisions, the almond, plum, peach and cherry; and so great is the choice that I think the best way to select the tree that most takes your fancy is to go and see it first in flower in a large park or garden, or in one of the big nurseries. In that way you can get a real feel for the plant, something never quite attained from however good an illustration in a book.

I must straightaway own up to a preference for the lovely winter-flowering Autumn Cherry, *P. subhirtella* 'Autumnalis' because although it is not so spectacular, or as densely covered with rich blossom as the spring-flowering prunus trees are, to have branches strung with pale pink flowers whenever there is a mild spell during the depths of winter, as this one does, makes it, I think, of special value to the tree scene in a garden. Then all spring and summer it is dressed in bright green foliage, a good background to the many colours of any other plants flowering around it.

I have a fully grown tree which has reached its full height of 30 ft (10 m) and which I also planted 30 years ago — on a slope so that the flowers can be seen from below against a blue sky. At the top of the rockery and in front of a bay window I have a half-standard so that the sight of this can be enjoyed from the house, when the weather is too unpleasant to venture out. On the edge of the back lawn, but at the foot of the terrace, I have a full standard which makes a nice round-headed tree about 12 ft (4 m) high and the nearby dividing low wall has been a protection for the trunk of the tree which would otherwise have grown like the leaning tower of Pisa, away from the prevailing, and very powerful, westerly wind off the sea.

These three trees, very different in stature, make a basic frame to the garden and can be relied on for flower at any time during the winter months. Any very exceptional cold snap will brown the blossoms, but with a rise of temperature the flowers bloom elsewhere along the branch, making a delicate tracery against a good background, so try to get an idea of what will best achieve this effect when you are selecting your planting site.

Two desirable varieties of this prunus are one that has a slightly darker pink flower, *P. subhirtella* 'Autumnalis Rosea'; and an elegant weeping form that blooms in March, *P. subhirtella* 'Pendula Rubra', with single deep rose-red blossoms massed along its arching stems, making a striking umbrella of rich colour. This needs to be carefully pruned to keep its shape, and within bounds if the planting area is restricted. But it will make a stunning display of shape and colour when grown as a specimen tree or feature in a larger garden.

Two other attractive trees to bloom early in the year are the Fuji Cherry, *P. incisa*, with the form 'Praecox' producing a cloud of white flowers, and 'February Pink' a similar display of blush-pink blooms closely packed along the branches. The serrated leaves turn a beautiful colour in autumn. *P. sargentii* is another one to do this, too, colouring orangey-red from its young bronzy leaves which appear after the single, cerise flowers have covered the branches. In the autumn it makes a real picture of flame, with its foliage set against the rich gleaming brown bark of this stunning tree.

The roots of these Flowering Cherries are said to be disrupting and intrusive, but I find that if they are carefully sited and any sign of roots surfacing dug out smartly, this risk is worth taking for the tremendous advantage of the graceful appearance of their beautiful flowers, especially in the drab days of winter. Nevertheless, don't ask for trouble by planting very near a drive or in a lawn which you do not want to see lifted. In rough grass they will look at their best and then not cause trouble to surrounding paths or shrubs by being planted too close to them. Choose an open site as they like plenty of sun and any good garden soil, preferably with a little lime, which is possibly why my three trees have prospered.

The Ornamental Peaches are tender and need to be sited where a wall or hedge will give some protection and provide a good background to the fragile, rose-pink flowers, which on *P. davidiana*, the Chinese Peach — introduced by the Abbé David in 1865 — can appear in January in favoured areas, holding back their flowering in colder parts of the country, so that the 1 in (2.5 cm) wide blooms are not so likely to be damaged by frost. It makes a small upright tree growing 12–20 ft (4–6 m) high, and there is a variety with white flowers

10 *Euchryphia x nymanensis* 'Nymansay': Nyman's Hybrid Eucryphia

11 *Halesia monticola vestita*: Mountain
Snowdrop Tree

12 *Hamamelis virginiana*: North American
Witch Hazel

13 *Koelreuteria paniculata*: Goldenrain Tree

14 *Liquidambar styraciflua* 'Lane Roberts':
Sweet or Red Gum Tree

but otherwise similar in growth, *P. davidiana* 'Alba'. The long graceful leaves are minutely toothed, giving an elegance of green all spring and summer.

The Ornamental Plums often have dark leaves and one of the most striking, *P. cerasifera* 'Pissardii', the Purple-leaved Plum, covers its stems with pink-budded white flowers at the end of March, a beautiful contrast against the rich foliage. After a good season small dark fruits appear, but I have only noticed them on my trees once or twice in the last 30 years, possibly because this tree comes from warmer climes. It was found by Pissard, a gardener to the Shah of Iran, over 100 years ago. Planted closely, this prunus can be developed into a very effective shrubby hedge and form a good wind-break.

The Common Almond, *P. dulcis*, will not produce edible almonds as far north as the British Isles. They ripen satisfactorily in the Mediterranean region, as far north as Bordeaux in France, and in similar climates, such as California in America; but they are grown in Britain for their ornamental qualities. The flowers are 1–2 in (2.5–5 cm) across, very conspicuous on the bare stems in March. There is a white-flowered variety, *P. dulcis* 'Alba', and an attractive slimly shaped tree with pink blooms on upright branches, *P. dulcis* 'Erecta', which would be ideal for a small space in a garden.

From a cross between an almond and a peach *P. × amygdalo-persica*, first mentioned in the seventeenth century, a cultivar was produced in Australia early in the 1900s, with large strong pink blooms. This is *P. × amygdalo-persica* 'Pollardii' a most desirable tree and so very effective when its pink-clothed branches can be seen against a bright sky in early spring.

Similarly, another cross between the Japanese Apricot *P. mume* 'Alphandii' and the Purple-leaved Plum *P. cerasifera* 'Pissardii' has given us the lovely *P. × blireana* with double pink blooms in April followed by shining bronze foliage, and the flowers are said to have a slight scent, though I find this is often blown away by the wind; though the blooms are, certainly, thickly massed on the branches in a veritable sea of pink.

Finally, there is a beautiful evergreen prunus — the so-called Flowering Cherries being largely deciduous — the Portugal Laurel, *P. lusitanica*. The long, slimly oval, toothed leaves are dark green and glossy but the racemes of flowers which come in June are even longer than the leaves and hawthorn-scented. I saw two very elegant trees about 30 ft (10 m) high decorating a garden in Surrey and covered with these conspicuous creamy blooms; they had been planted by the owner of the house many years ago. When young this prunus is shrubby in form and will make a very good hedge, being particularly useful as it will grow in total shade. The bark is smooth and almost black, and the leaf-stalks maroon, giving a very luxurious look, with the addition of red fruits later which turn very much darker when fully ripe. It will grow in any soil, even on poor chalk, so it is a good tree to bear in mind when choosing a feature for the garden. Being evergreen it remains constantly decorative. There is a very attractive variety *P. lusitanica* 'Myrtifolia' which would be suitable where space is limited as it does not grow above 15 ft (5 m) and has a decidedly upright habit, being solid, neat and conical in form, with smaller narrower and longer leaves. This variety is recommended as a good substitute in areas too cold to support the bay tree. But take care not to overclip this prunus or the lovely effect will be spoiled.

PTELEA

The name ptelea, derived from the Greek name for elm — the seeds of both trees being similar — is a small genus of deciduous large shrubs or low-growing trees introduced from the eastern part of North America, but naturalised in Central Europe. They are well worth growing as they are hardy, even in Zone 4, and easy as to most positions and soil, preferring some shade.

P. trifoliata, the leaves having three leaflets, known as the Hop Tree or Swamp Dogwood, is a special attraction in June and July when it produces heads of small but exceptionally strongly scented dull-white flowers, followed by large bunches of fruits in the form of slim discs. This is one of the trees from the large rue family — another being the citrus — and all parts of it are highly aromatic.

The shiny leaves turn gold before they fall, though there is a form with yellow leaves, *P. trifoliata* 'Aurea', but I think it gives more variety to have the green first and then the change of colour.

The form of this tree is to grow slowly to between 10–20 ft (3–6 m), rarely more, with expanding branches from a short, sometimes bent trunk; so if you prefer a more upright shape, plant *P. trifoliata* 'Fastigiata', where the branches grow more erectly.

This would be a useful tree to have in a walled town garden as it likes to be in a little shade, and the powerful scent of the flowers would be even more heady, trapped inside an enclosed area.

PTEROCARYA

The pterocarya or Wing Nut is from a group of quick-growing deciduous trees belonging to the walnut and hickory family. With their large pinnate leaves they make very graceful specimens for the park or garden, with long inflorescences which, from a distance, give them the appearance of wisteria. *P. fraxinifolia*, from the Caucasus and Iran, reaches about 35 ft (11 m) in 20 years, becoming a wide head of branches on a short rough trunk. A fine sight in isolation, it is even more vigorous, suckering freely and growing into thickets when planted in groups along the banks of a river as it likes moist soil so long as it is not ill-drained. It would be an ideal tree for planting some way from the house, perhaps on the edge of a pond.

The feature of the flowers are the length of the green catkins, the female ones being four or five times longer than the male, these being at least 4 in (10 cm). The catkins are followed by decorative strings of winged fruits, the tiny nuts, which are more abundant after a hot summer.

P. stenoptera, the Chinese Wing Nut, grows to a similar height but the leaves and catkins are not so long and it is not as hardy as *P. fraxinifolia*, only to Zone 6 instead of Zone 5.

But a cross between these two varieties *P.* × *rehderiana* is perhaps the most desirable to choose, tolerating the hardier Zone number and not growing quite so tall eventually, yet the faster-growing when young. The attractive catkins, and then the strings of fruit-nuts, remain for an even longer time decorating the tree and making this a most desirable and uncommon addition to any garden.

PYRUS

The ornamental pear is a very delightful tree to plant in the garden, particularly *P. salicifolia* 'Pendula' the Weeping Willow-leaved Pear, which originated from the Caucasus but is hardy in Zone 4 though it does not like shade and requires a sunny site in a good neutral soil. I visited a garden once where this tree had been beautifully trained by thinning it close to the rough stem of its trunk, so that the silvery pendulous branches hung in graceful arches to the ground. For, if left unpruned, this tree becomes too thick and untidy. But it doesn't grow too tall, so is ideal for placing strategically in the garden, centred on the lawn, or it can look lovely combined with moving water, from a nearby stream or a little waterfall where small pools are set one below the other. Then the slim silvery-grey leaves are seen to best advantage. In April it produces clusters of creamy flowers decorating the arched branches. Gradually the leaves lose a slight furriness they have at first and become shiny, green, and less silvery.

This is a good tree for a small town garden and it is the neatest weeping tree. It is tolerant of a dry situation as well as a moist one, its only requirement being a good helping of sun. Though the blossoms are pear-like and plentiful, the resultant small brown conical fruits are not pleasant to eat.

Another pyrus *P. nivalis*, but from Southern Europe, taller and slimmer than the weeping variety, has broader leaves that are white and downy. They appear with the flowers, again in April, and they become grey as they age. This is not quite so hardy, only to Zone 5, but it makes a fine tree if you have room to grow it. When loaded with its clear-white blooms in spring, it can be a wonderful sight. Though the fruits are also small and insignificant, they do become sweet and edible eventually.

QUERCUS

This is a genus of over 400 species, and more than 200 of these, with their numerous varieties and forms, are known in Great Britain. Nearly all of them are hardy, both evergreen and deciduous. The oaks form one of the largest genera in the world, widely spread, but missing in Australasia and most of Africa other than the northern part. Of the same family as the beech, forests of both these trees abounded in Europe before the age of man. But most of the oaks become far too large in height and spread for the average garden, though if you can find room, it is a noble tree to grow for posterity, and the grandchildren will appreciate your forethought in planting and cherishing something from which they will get the full enjoyment and benefit.

Perhaps the most well known is *Q. robur*, the Common Oak or English Oak, the most widely grown in England, liking a rich deep soil, long-lived, possibly up to 800 years or more, slow to mature, with a stout short trunk and wide spread of branches. It tolerates Zone 5, and the next most familiar oak, *Q. petraea*, the Sessile Oak or Durmast Oak, also very long-lived, is slightly hardier to Zone 4 and stands up to exposed coastal winds and damper conditions. It is grown a lot in the West of England and in France. The spring foliage of these two oaks is olive-green and a pale yellowy-bronze, turning a tawny-buff and rusty-copper in autumn, those of *Q. petraea* being slightly larger on long stalks, with sessile acorns, whereas *Q. robur* is exactly the opposite, the leaves unstalked and the fruits or acorns on a slender stalk. So this is an easy way to tell the difference between these two trees, both of which flower in May and have timber much prized for furniture-making.

These two species have several varieties, some of which are suitable for planting in the garden. *Q. robur* 'Concordia', the Golden Oak, is also slow-growing but eventually only becoming small and round-headed in shape with chrome-yellow leaves all spring and summer. *Q. robur* 'Fastigiata', the Cypress Oak, develops a fine columnar shape with upright branches, but does grow quite large, and the better choice would be the form *Q. robur* 'Fastigiata Purpurea' which is much smaller and with attractive purple leaves; or another elegant shape, *Q. robur* 'Pendula', the Weeping Oak, is a small graceful pendulously branched tree.

The Turkey Oak, *Q. cerris*, slightly more tender from Zone 6 and Asia Minor and Southern Europe, is about the fastest-growing, and suitable for a chalky soil but far too vast for the average garden, though it could be planted at the edge of a property near the sea, because it stands up well to gales. It is usually grown for its ornamental properties, as the timber is inferior, being liable to split; but the decorative acorn cups are covered with cylindrical scales like coarse moss.

Two species that will not tolerate chalk and like a lime-free neutral soil are *Q. coccinea*, the Scarlet Oak, again making a large tree, from the eastern United States and south-eastern Canada and Zone 4, with first yellow, then glossy green leaves, turning a brilliant scarlet in autumn in its native areas, though a little unreliable in colour in Britain. The leaves turn gradually, branch by branch, and some remain on the tree half-way through the winter. The clone *Q. coccinea* 'Splendens', does give a more regular fine red coloration; the Pin Oak, *Q. palustris*, from the same area of the United States and Canada and also a lime-hater, with shiny, yellow then green leaves but smaller than the Scarlet Oak, turns an even lovelier red in autumn. The two trees form an important part of the wonderful colour display of the American 'Fall'. The variety *Q. palustris* 'Pendula' would make an agreeable weeping form to add to the design of any garden, as the shape of the Pin Oak, anyway, is pyramidal with branches that hang down at the tips. *Q. palustris* prefers wet sites, so planted on the edge of a pond or river it should do well.

The Red Oak, *Q. rubra*, again from the eastern United States and Zone 4, likes similar soil but grows to a huge broad-headed tree, even in industrial areas. The leaves are dull-green, unlike the glossy ones of *Q. coccinea*, but it colours beautifully in autumn, particularly on an acid soil, producing a mixture of red, yellow and russet tones. The timber is hard but not durable and principally of use as firewood, though the bark is used for tanning leather being rich in tannin, as, indeed, are *Q. robur* and *Q. petraea*. The form *Q. rubra* 'Aurea' makes a much smaller tree and if you can find a site in half-shade with other shrubs and trees around to give protection, the leaves will keep their rich yellow colour, as

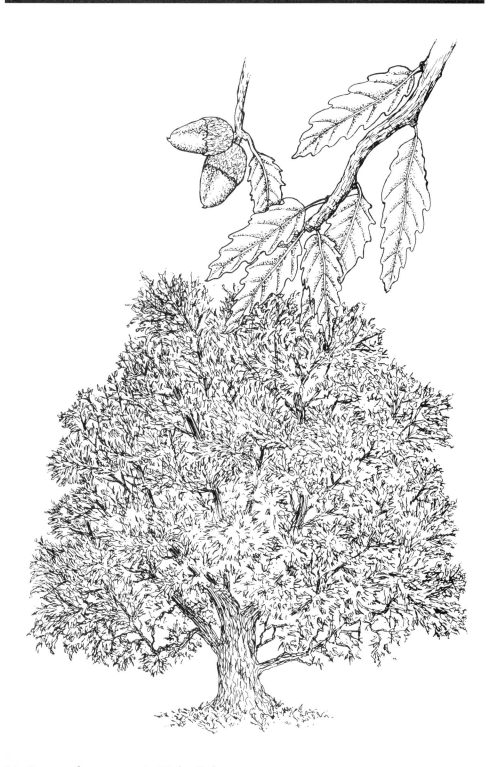

22 *Quercus ilex gramuntia*: Holm Oak

strong sun scorches them. Through the summer they become touched with green, finally becoming entirely so before falling. The acorns of *Q. rubra* stay two years on the tree and after they fall lie till spring before germinating.

My favourites are the evergreen oaks, with their dense black-green leaves. The best known of these is perhaps the Holm Oak, Holly Oak or Evergreen Oak, *Q. ilex*, a native of the Mediterranean region, where it is an important shade and timber tree, but only in Zone 7–8, so it is not for every area in Britain, particularly those that are cold and inland. It has a lovely bark, grey and smooth when young, then becoming rough and cracked into small squares, and almost black in colour. Though it does grow, it left unchecked, to a very large tree with a good spread — there is a specimen not far from where I live at least 80 ft (25 m) high dominating the sky above the lovely old house beneath its branches — it will stand clipping well and can be trained and kept to a small size very successfully. And it makes an excellent hedge, giving protection to a garden against sea winds. One variety *Q. ilex gramuntia* has sharply-toothed leaves and grows very slowly to make a compact, shrubby form, a good example of an oak that can be grown in quite a small area, and *Q. ilex* will stand shade, too, which is useful when choosing a site in the garden. It flowers, with sprays of yellow male catkins, when the often reddish young leaves appear in June, the female flowers being in the new leaf axils. The acorns fall in October and are always very numerous after a good summer. Pigs are very fond of them and they give a special flavour to their meat.

There are several other evergreen oaks that often only make a small tree in Britain, though growing to a larger size in their native habitat. *Q. alnifolia*, the Golden Oak from Cyprus, can be shrubby in form with hard green shiny leaves and furry yellow undersides. It is slow-growing and if given some protection from cold winds is quite hardy in the southern areas of England.

Q. coccifera, the Kermes Oak or Holly Oak from the Mediterranean and particularly Portugal, is very slow-growing and forms a dense neat tree with small shiny variable leaves, occasionally prickly and at other times smooth and flat. The new leaves in spring are hairy and bronze-coloured and come at the same time as the catkins. The fruit does not ripen till the second year and is found among the older leaves. The acorn cup is covered in very prickly scales. This small tree is tender and can only be grown in very mild areas of Great Britain, but it is lovely to see, dark and green, growing over the hot dry hills of the Mediterranean. Its name comes from the Kermes insect which inhabits the tree and from which the dye cochineal is extracted.

Q. suber, the Cork Oak, is very long-lived and comes from the same area and also North Africa, but can be found as far east as western Yugoslavia. The rough thick short-stemmed bark is spongy, the top layer being removed to use for cork. This is done every 8–10 years leaving a pinky under-bark, which darkens in time. This stripping does not seem to affect the trees adversely, some of which have withstood this treatment for nearly 500 years. The dark green polished leaves are felty grey underneath. It needs Zone 8 so it is hardly grown at all in Northern Europe or Great Britain, because it must have strong sun and won't tolerate any exposure to cold. It will grow 12 ft (4 m) in 20 years and can reach 60 ft (18 m) when mature.

Q. × turneri is an attractive cross of the deciduous *Q. robur* and the evergreen *Q. ilex* and makes an ideal tree for the garden with its compact, round-headed shape of black-green leaves, 2½–4½ in (6–11 cm) long, which do not fall till early spring. It is very hardy and happy on even chalky soil.

All the oaks have differently shaped leaves, large and small, slim and willow-like, others oval and some lobed; they can be dull or glossy, toothed or wavy-edged, and vary in size from tiny to several inches in length. The male and female flowers are separate on the same tree, males in slender catkins, females in a group, or sometimes single, and these develop into acorns. The size, shape, texture and colour of the acorns vary considerably.

Propagate from fresh acorns in autumn before they have had a chance to dry out, though clones such as *Q. coccinea* 'Splendens' must be propagated vegetatively. Make sure to choose the right site, as their long tap root means even little plants do not move well. This strong root anchors them firmly in the soil, so that they are not so likely to be affected by ordinary gales as some trees are. Though in the freak conditions like those in the October 1987 hurricane in Southern England, even this strong root will not protect them.

Pruning is not necessary, other than training a straight, non-forking lead; but take off any damaged or dead branches in winter.

RHODODENDRON

In the Himalayas the *Rhododendron arboreum* grows to 50 ft (15 m) or more. This species was the first one to be introduced and is the parent of many of the hundreds of hybrids we can now have in our gardens. The majority of them are shrubs but, given the right conditions, *R. arboreum* will attain tree-size in Britain. It is evergreen and such a magnificent tree with its huge dark green leathery leaves, 8 in (20 cm) long, the undersides hairy and a curious white or rusty-brown. The heads of stunning 2 in (5 cm) long bell-like flowers are at least 6 in (15 cm) across. The blooms can be a rich crimson, *R. arboreum* 'Blood Red'; a pure-white, *R. arboreum* 'Album'; or a strong pink, attractively spotted a darker shade, *R. arboreum* 'Roseum'.

In Zone 6 and where it can be given shelter from strong winds which damage the massive leaves, and where its flowers can have some protection from injurious frosts — as it starts to flower in January in ideal conditions, though usually around March — it grows to a great size over the years. I have seen many fine trees in Sussex flowering profusely in ideal semi-woodland conditions. They require an acid soil, moist and peaty like all rhododendrons, and a humid atmosphere. Though not flowering when very young, it is, I think, worth being patient in order to see the fantastic blooms when they finally come, early one spring.

The best method of propagation is by layering in July or August.

RHUS

The Rhus or Sumach is a member of the Cashew family and composed of a

23 *Rhus trichocarpa*: Sumach

genus of over 200 trees and shrubs, deciduous and evergreen, which includes various poisonous species, the American poison ivy being the best known.

But a good tree to grow for the average garden is the deciduous (sometimes semi-evergreen) Stag's-horn Sumach or Vinegar Tree, *R. typhina*, from Eastern North America, which is so-called because the extraordinary thick and pithy branches, with their mat of browny-red hairs when young, do look like the horns of a stag. It does not make a very big tree, about 25 ft (8 m), but the large pinnate leaves, downy at first and divided into 11–31 lanceolate toothed leaflets, are the main feature, turning the most wonderful colours in autumn, ranging from yellow, orange to red and purple. The inconspicuous greeny-white male and female flowers appear on separate trees, opening in late June or July, in clusters at the ends of the shoots; the male being larger, but the female blooms develop into showy brownish-crimson fruits 4–8 in (10–20 cm) long like bristly red fir cones, remaining throughout the winter. The female form *R. typhina* 'Laciniata' has the same large leaves but they are deeply gashed, giving them a delicate fern-like appearance and turning an even brighter orange and yellow.

R. trichocarpa has downy leaves which are coppery-pink at first then green and becoming a rich orange in autumn. The fruits hang down in yellow clusters. This tree is a native of China, Korea and Japan.

The Varnish or Lacquer Tree, *R. verniciflua*, native to China, Himalaya and Japan, has leaves 1–2 ft (30–60 cm) long, composed of 7–13 leaflets each 4–7 in (10–18 cm) in length. These are downy beneath, and open sprays of ¼ in (0.6 cm) flowers appear in July, followed by yellow-brown fruits, nothing like the grand ones of *R. typhina*; and the leaves do not colour quite so well in autumn as the other two. But this deciduous tree, *R. verniciflua*, is famous for the poisonous irritant juice which is extracted from the stem and made into dyes and black varnish used in the manufacture of lacquer in China and Japan. In China the oil from the fruits was used to make candles. This tree will reach 60 ft (18 m) in its native habitat, and around two thirds of that height in Britain.

The sumachs are all hardy in Zone 5, and easy as to soil — in fact a poor one seems to give better autumn colour — and they like a sunny site. If the tree is not grafted, the suckers it produces, particularly around *R. typhina*, can be dug up and potted on in the autumn; otherwise take root cuttings in March; or preferably layer the branches then.

In February prune by cutting back any branches that have grown too long, in order to keep the tree's shape fairly upright and dense. Some stems can be cut back to within 1 ft (30 cm) of the ground and then the new growth tends to produce even larger leaves. But this, of course, encourages a shrubby habit.

The sumach makes a fantastic display in the garden, with its showy and unusual fruits and leaves; and it is very tolerant of any soil and is not affected by city pollution.

ROBINIA

Robinia, known as the Black Locust Tree and related to Gleditsia, the Honey Locust, is a genus of about 20 deciduous species, all fast-growing and native to northern Mexico and the United States of America; but now found not only in Europe and Australasia but in many other areas of the world. They are easy to grow in any soil, but prefer chalk and sandy ones. They tolerate the atmospheric pollution in cities well and therefore are useful for town and park plantings. The bark is extremely rugged and deeply furrowed, a rich dark brown. They are very beautiful trees, with pinnate leaves and hanging groups of pea-shaped flowers, like wisteria, pink, pale mauve or white, depending on the species. The fruits are seeds in a flat brown pod. They all need to be planted in full sun, in order to flower well, with some protection from strong winds as their wood is very brittle. If the soil is dry and poor they do better than in a rich one, which will produce lush growth more liable to break. To save the loss of branches, however, rampant shoots are best shortened to avoid any damage, and trim out old flowering wood as the flowers fade in summer.

The species most often grown, with a suckering habit and at least 16 varieties — many of these without spines — is *R. pseudoacacia*, the Common Acacia, False Acacia or Black Locust from Zone 3 and the eastern part of the United States, found in the Appalachian Mountains from Pennsylvania to Georgia, where it reaches 80 ft (25 m) in height, though half that height in England. The wood is very hard, a lovely greenish ochre-tinted colour. It doesn't disintegrate in the soil, so is useful for fencing. It has scented white flowers in June, touched with yellow at the base of the upper petal. The fruit pods are 2–4 in (5–10 cm) long enclosing kidney-shaped seeds. The light green leaves are oval, opposite and hairy when young, composed of 13–15 leaflets, spiny at the tips. The twigs also have short stout spines.

This tree is now widely planted all over Europe, for it likes to have well-drained soil and will stand dry places, the blooms being especially attractive to bees. Keep the trunk to a single leader when young to prevent forking, for the branches will become twisted and crooked as they age, giving the tree a very picturesque outline. The form *R. pseudoacacia* 'Frisia' is a much smaller tree with scarlet spines and chrome-yellow foliage from spring through to the autumn. So when thinking of colour combinations and shapes of leaves for the garden, the bright leaves of this variety will give a cheerful uplift to the overall picture, particularly when the sun is shining through it. Or if space is very limited, *R. pseudoacacia* 'Pyramidalis' does not grow too tall and forms a slim column of spineless erect branches. *R. pseudoacacia* 'Semperflorens' is very attractive as it goes on producing its graceful sprays of flowers throughout the summer, particularly when it is a fine warm one.

I have seen *R. pseudoacacia* growing in a small garden and kept to a manageable size for its surroundings by pruning three times during the growing season. This species is called pseudoacacia because it looks rather like the true acacia, which, of course, is really the Mimosa or Wattle.

R. kelseyi from North Carolina grows to about 12 ft (4 m) and produces pinky-lilac flowers in June, followed by bristly pods. The leaves are divided into 9–11 leaflets. This is a very elegant species, shrub-like at first, then a small tree with slim branches and graceful foliage.

R. viscosa, known as the Clammy Locust because of its sticky leaf-stalks and young shoots, which have some thorns, is a native of Carolina and Zone 3, and now found in eastern areas of the United States. It grows to about 35–40 ft (11–12 m). The abundant flowers come in May or June, a lovely pale pink, touched at the base with yellow, but they have little scent. The narrow fruit-pods, 2–3 in (5–8 cm) long, are covered with sticky hairs and enclose reddish seeds. The leaves are 7–12 in (18–30 cm) long, composed of 13–21 leaflets on a hairy, sticky main stem, the branchlets being dark reddish-brown. This species flowers well when quite young.

A nice cross between *R. pseudoacacia* and *R. viscosa*, *R.* × *ambigua*, has attractive pale pink blooms in June and sticky young shoots. It only grows to quite a small tree and the one to choose for the garden is *R.* × *ambigua*

'Bella-rosea' where the shoots are even stickier and the flowers larger and a lovely deep rich pink. All the leaves of the robinia species become a beautiful pale gold before falling.

Propagate from seed for the true species, but suckers which the varieties produce can be tipped and grown on in the autumn.

SALIX

The Salix or willow is a genus of around 500 very hardy and mostly deciduous species, all fast-growing and very decorative; whether they are tiny prostrate forms or enormous trees, they are attractive in their weeping state, or when they have brightly coloured bark or hung with beautiful silvery catkins, like those of the Pussy Willow.

Willows are easy to grow in a rich deep loam, many of them preferring damp situations and they look most effective in association with ponds or rivers, where their graceful often pendulous form can be reflected in the water. However, the miniature alpine species like a drier and slightly more acid soil. All the willows prefer a sunny site, but the roots travel far, so plant well away from a building or garden wall.

The miniature form is *S. repens*, the Creeping Willow from Europe, growing only a few inches high and spreading along the ground, very attractive in a rockery with its erect branches of tiny elliptical and shiny grey leaves touched with silver, and little catkins covering the bare branches in spring which go a lovely bronze after having been fertilised. The form *S. repens argentea* is semi-prostrate and found by the sea in sandy soil. This can be grown as a standard and makes a charming miniature weeping tree, whereas the other forms are really shrubs.

S. alba, the White Willow, is perhaps the most well known of our native willows, found all over Europe and into northern Asia and even North Africa. It is often to be seen beside rivers and canals but is tough enough to act as a wind-break near the sea. It likes sandy moist soil, not a chalky shallow one. It will grow to 80 ft (25 m), slender in form with a stout trunk and very hardy to Zone 2 with a cloud of slim silvery tapering leaves, which turn yellow in autumn. The catkins make a show in late April, at the same time as the leaves, the males, on separate trees, yellow and $1\frac{1}{2}$–2 in (4–5 cm) long, the females green and about the same size, and these ripen to become fruiting catkins, which in June split open to release their white tufted seeds. The bark of the trunk is grey and cracks with age.

For the garden, some of the varieties are smaller, with lovely coloured barks. *S. alba* 'Sericea' is much slower in growth, and in form, with even more vivid silvery leaves. Very effective and showy. *S. alba* 'Chermesina', the Scarlet Willow, has gorgeous scarlety-orange bark which looks very dramatic in winter after the leaves have fallen. To prevent its growing too tall it is best hard-pruned at least every other year in early spring, and this encourages the growth of strong and even brighter young branches which can be admired close to *S. alba* 'Vitellina', the Golden Willow, is similar to the latter and needs the same treatment, but the branches are a sharp chrome-yellow. There are only male trees of this variety and it does not grow so rapidly.

The famous Weeping Willow, *S. babylonica* from China and Zone 6, is a little tender for some sites, and liable to disease, and the hybrid that is most often grown now is *S. × chrysocoma*, the Golden Weeping Willow, which tolerates Zone 2. From a broad dome-shaped head its graceful buff-yellow branches hang to the ground with their lance-shaped leaves. The flowers, opening in April, have the same colour catkins as *S. alba* but are only ¾ in (2 cm) long, usually male, but sometimes male and female flowers occur in the same catkin. The bright green leaves are narrow and are covered in silky hairs, hairless when mature, about 3–6 in (8–15 cm) long, a lovely dark green with paler undersides. The new shoots are brown and hang down gracefully. These shoots and the branches eventually become golden. But it can grow to rather a large tree, so must be given plenty of space.

S. caprea, the Goat Willow, Pussy Willow or Great Sallow, is a small tree from Western Asia and Europe. The dark green leaves are quite broad for a willow, rather wrinkled, and hairy underneath, on red downy stems. The flowers come on separate trees in March, the males silky and grey and turning a lovely yellow and often called Palm; and the females, which are known as the Pussy Willow, are silvery and develop green capsules which in May release white tufted seeds. The young shoots have grey hairs when new and then become a glossy brownish-red. The bark is smooth and grey, gradually turning brown and fissured. This tree can grow too large for the average garden and can be pruned hard, but the form known as the Kilmarnock Willow, *S. caprea* 'Pendula', makes a better choice, being an elegant tree about 12 ft (4 m) high with a neat weeping crown. It is a female clone so does not have the bright catkins of the male but, nevertheless, is such a desirable size and shape that it is worth considering.

S. daphnoides, the Violet Willow, native to Scandinavia but widely planted in Central Asia and the Himalayas and Northern Europe and Zone 4, is a delightful colour with its violet young shoots covered with a greyish-white bloom. Again like the coloured varieties of *S. alba*, it is best hard-pruned regularly and then gives a very effective fan-shaped display in winter; or it can be grown as a small standard, the shoots being pollarded every year to the base of the crown. But if left alone it will grow to an upright tree 30 ft (10 m) in height. The catkins come on the naked branches in late winter before the leaves, the males fluffy and silvery turning yellow, the females smaller. The female trees are also slimmer in shape than the male. The form *S. daphnoides* 'Aglaia' is the best to plant as it is a male clone and possesses the large yellow catkins. When planted near water and pruned hard, the purple-violet stems are very striking. The leaves are lance-shaped to oval with glandular teeth and a rich glossy green, glaucous beneath. These trees are used for cutting osiers — called 'Violets' in the trade — for basket-making.

S. matsudana, the Pekin Willow from Korea and North China and Manchuria, grows into a reasonable-sized tree of a pleasant conical shape with slim green leaves, grey underneath, covering the slender stems. The young stems mature to a yellow colour. The catkins come at the same time as the leaves

24 *Salix daphnoides* 'Aglaia': Violet Willow

in spring. The female tree is the one most often grown. Being of Zone 4 it will tolerate dry and inhospitable sites exposed to the cold. There are two elegant varieties; *S. matsudana* 'Pendula', a beautiful weeping tree and more resistant to disease than *S. × chrysocoma* which it resembles, though not making quite such a stunning display; the second is *S. matsudana* 'Tortuosa', the Contorted Willow or Corkscrew Willow, which looks quite extraordinary, particularly in winter when the filigree of twisted branches makes a frame against the sky. The twigs and long narrow waxy olive-green leaves are also oddly curled and any straight branches should be removed to keep the corkscrew effect. The female catkins, about 1 in (2.5 cm) long, come in April and develop into fruiting catkins, releasing their white cottony seeds in June. This tree makes an interesting focal point in the garden, especially if you are aiming for a Japanese effect, growing eventually and quite quickly to about 40–50 ft (12–15 m).

S. pentandra, the Bay Willow or Laurel-leaved Willow from Europe and northern Asia, grows wild in the North of England, but is planted elsewhere, particularly when a bay tree is found to be too tender, as this willow tolerates Zone 4 and is much planted in Norway. It makes a small tree with large, glossy and yellow winter buds and the leaves are unlike any other willow in having no grey colouring but are a dark lustrous green and slightly sticky, 2–4 in (5–10 cm) long and pointed, but much broader than most other willows. They give off a delightful aroma as they open, or when crushed. The catkins come in late spring with the leaves, the females green, the males larger and a rich chrome-yellow. The fruiting catkins can be 4 in (10 cm) long, releasing their cottony seeds in June.

S. triandra, the Almond-leaved Willow or French Willow from Europe to eastern Asia in Zone 4, is a very desirable small tree to grow, reaching only about 30 ft (10 m) and with the most delightful male catkins which are fragrant and stand upright, slender and yellow, rather like a mimosa bloom. The leaves come at the same time and are very narrow, glossy, and have serrated edges. The twigs are reddish-brown or greeny. This species is easily recognized by its peeling, flaky bark, and the stems are often used for basket-making.

S. purpurea, the Purple Osier, found all over Europe and in Central Asia, is rather shrubby in habit but can be grown on a single stem, so developing a graceful arching shape of purple branches, the young shoots being yellow beneath the bark. The slender catkins come in April strung along the stems, often in pairs, before the slim waxy greeny-blue hairless leaves appear. Its flexible branches are, also, used in basket-making. This tree will grow well on wet or dry ground. *S. purpurea* 'Pendula', the American Weeping Willow, is a delightful weeping form, especially when trained as a standard, when it is ideal for the smaller garden.

Many species of willow have barks from which salicyclic acid is obtained. This has similar properties to quinine and is the active pain-killing ingredient of aspirin.

This is just a selection of the many willow species that appeal to me, but there are dozens more attractive forms, of great height and grace, or miniatures which can decorate a rockery. Unfortunately, many of them are subject to canker or scab. But all are easy to propagate from November to February, in ordinary soil by striking 1 ft (30 m) cuttings; or they can be grown from 'setts', that is, a piece of branch 6–8 ft (2–2.5 m) long, one-third of which should be buried firmly in the ground, in the place where you want the tree to grow. And, unlike other trees, willows do well when planted deeply, so that the lower part of the trunk is buried. As the majority of willows are unisexual, the male forms must be ordered if you are planting for maximum catkin effect.

Apart from pruning the coloured-stemmed varieties each spring to improve bark colour, the ordinary willows can be thinned occasionally, or they can be pollarded to several feet high, or coppiced: that is, cut to ground level.

SASSAFRAS

Sassafras is a difficult tree to establish and best planted when very young, straight from a pot into its permanent position. But it is quite hardy to Zone 4 when well established, though not always long-lived. It is composed of a small genus of only three species, all deciduous, and requiring soil completely free of lime, and very well-drained.

S. albidum's greatest attribute is the delightfully scented foliage, the young bark and leaves having a powerful aromatic fragrance. This, and the roots, produce an oil once used in pharmacy and now chiefly in perfumery, or to make the pink Sassafras tea. The leaves have a pleasant tang and the Choctaw Indians made soap from them.

The flowers are small but in yellowy-green clusters which appear in May. The male and female flowers are on separate trees, the male insignificant. When the female fruit ripens it produces from the calyx a glossy rich blue drupe attached to an equally gleaming red stalk. Sassafras is unusual in that although it is a member of the bay family and aromatic, yet it is deciduous. The leaves are rather extraordinary, being variously shaped on the same tree, some oval, others with two or three lobes, but all with wedge-shaped bases, and a pale shiny green, glaucous beneath. Then in September, before they fall, they turn a soft yellow in Europe and a rich orangey-crimson in the States.

Sassafras produces a nice straight rugged trunk and develops into an elegant conical shape, the flexuous branches short compared to its height. But it never grows very tall in Europe, preferring the greater variation between the extremely hot summers and cold winters of North America.

Propagate from seed or from root suckers, which are produced when the tree is well established. The ideal site is a woodland one, where the soil is warm and loamy and, even though it is quite hardy, there is some protection from the other trees.

SOPHORA

The sophoras are composed of a genus of around 50 species of evergreen and deciduous shrubs and trees of the pea family. Many of them are rather too tender for growing in anything but a temperate climate. They are found all around the Pacific, from the south-western states of America, Chile, New Zealand, Korea, Japan and China.

I have tried to grow *S. tetraptera*, a lovely evergreen from New Zealand, which does succeed inland in Sussex, but I don't think I gave it quite enough protection. It was planted against a southern wall, but exposed to cold sea winds which damaged the delicate pinnate sprays of grey-green leaflets — which increase in quantity as the tree ages — and the beautiful chrome-yellow clusters of pea-shaped flowers, 1–2 in (2.5–5 cm) long, hanging like elongated fleshy bells in May. It is seen at its best in its native habitat of New Zealand, where it is known by the Maori name, Kowhai, and is famous there as the national flower. (The name sophora is from an Arabic word.) It is not a large tree, growing to 30–40 ft (10–12 m), but where the region is colder than Zone 9, it tends to remain much smaller, but is a gorgeous sight against a very protected warm wall or trellis. The seed pods which follow the blooms are like a string of beads and have four unusually broad wings. There is a very desirable form *S. tetraptera* 'Grandiflora' with larger flowers and leaflets. The variety *S. tetraptera microphylla* has slightly smaller flowers and leaves, making a neater dense bush or small tree which is rather hardier than the type and found in Chile as well as New Zealand.

The commonest sophora is *S. japonica*, much hardier than *S. tetraptera* and deciduous, but it needs the dry Mediterranean type of climate to produce a good flowering in summer, and then only on older trees. For this reason it does best in the eastern parts of the British Isles, rather than the warmer but much moister western areas. Its name is misleading as it came originally from China, but was grown extensively in Japan and discovered by visiting Europeans and given the name Japanese Pagoda Tree or Scholar's Tree. As it ages its trunk forms grotesquely twisted shapes. In other ways it looks rather like a false acacia (Robinia), but does not have thorns, the bark is rough and the flowers — much smaller than *S. tetraptera* — are in erect sprays, in creamy-white or the palest pink 6–9 in (15–23 cm) long panicles, not opening until September and falling before they fade, making a creamy-pink carpet around the trunk. Then the following seed pods are flat. It grows very tall but prunes well to a more desirable height for planting in gardens and parks, and for gracefully lining avenues. The glossy rich green pointed leaves are hairy or downy underneath. The fruit and the flowers possess a yellow colouring matter.

S. japonica 'Pendula' is a very attractive form which, if grown in the centre of a lawn, provides welcome shade as its hanging leaves bend to touch the grass. In a dry position this tree is much more effective than a weeping willow.

S. affinis is a native of Arkansas and Texas and though introduced into England in the last century has not often been planted here since. It is an ideal tree for the small garden, forming a nice round head with delicate pinnate leaves and pinkish blooms during June.

Sophoras are all great sun-lovers and will grow in any type of soil which is of good quality and well-drained. They can be propagated from either seed or cuttings.

SORBUS

The sorbus is a very decorative genus of trees of around 100 species which are ideal for the garden, as their average height is 30–60 ft (10–18 m) and they are all hardy and happy in any fertile well-drained soil, in a sunny position. They fall into three groups, most of them in two, the Whitebeam, and the Rowan or Mountain Ash. In the first the leaves are simple, and lobed or toothed; in the second, the trees have pinnate leaves with many leaflets. Most of them flower in May, with bunches of small white flowers among the attractive leaves, followed by clusters of bright edible berries about the size of a pea.

I mention here a good choice for the garden of various sizes and shapes of tree — though most have an erect habit — the fruits being from white, to yellow, orange, bright red, deep red and brown. These berries are loved by the birds who eat the red first and leave the orange till later and the paler colours to the end of winter, so giving themselves a constant supply. Therefore it is a good idea, if you have room to plant more than one tree, to choose those with different berries, and then in a cold winter the birds in your garden will be assured of some food to help them through the bitter weather.

S. alnifolia the Whitebeam from Japan, Korea, Manchuria and China and Zone 5, makes a small slender upright tree with shiny leaves like those of the alder or hornbeam, strongly veined and double-toothed, nearly 3 in (8 cm) long, green and then scarlet and orange in autumn. The fruits are oval and a bright red, and ½ in (1.2 cm) long, speckled with black dots and said to look like ladybirds.

S. americana, the American Mountain Ash from the Eastern United States and Zone 2, prefers an acid soil and makes a small erect tree with long red gummy buds in early spring. The leaflets of the ash-grey pinnate 10 in (25 cm) long leaves are toothed and become a tawny-orange in autumn. The brilliant red berries are small, but in large clusters and rich in vitamins. This is a slow-growing tree, eventually making 15–30 ft (5–10 m).

S. aria, the Whitebeam from Europe and Zone 5, is a tough little tree tolerating wind and air pollution and often found on chalky and limestone soils, particularly in the South of England. It forms a neat round-headed pyramid-shaped tree growing to about 30–40 ft (10–12 m) with bunches of richly scented flowers in May, which become green, then deep red berries, large and dotted with brown specks in autumn. The grey bark has white patches when young, becoming red-brown. The green leaves are obovate and irregularly toothed and whitened by a thick down at first all over, the uppers gradually losing this and showing their bright green colouring. By the autumn they have turned a gorgeous golden-russet. The berries can be used for distillation, as their flesh is floury and sweet. A very pretty little weeping form, ideal for the small garden as it only grows to 9 ft (2.7 m), is *S. aria* 'Pendula' with much tinier and slimmer leaves.

S. domestica, the Service Tree from Zone 5 and Western Asia, Southern Europe and North Africa, grows slowly to around 50 ft (15 m) with spreading branches of 8 in (20 cm) long pinnate leaves, yellowish above and with hairs beneath. The bark is brown and orange, rough and cracked. The buds are bright green and sticky. The flowers open in May in 4 in (10 cm) clusters of small ½ in (1.2 cm) blooms. The fruits which follow are about 1–1½ in (2.5–4 cm) long, oval or rounded, and green touched with red and yellow. When ripe, which can

25 *Sorbus* 'Joseph Rock': Rowan; and *S.* 'Embley': Chinese Scarlet Rowan

be any time between August and February, they go brown and are then edible and are used in various ways, including in the making of a type of beer. Like the fruit of the Medlar (*Mespilus germanica*) (see Chapter 2), it needs to be half rotten or 'bletted' before it is palatable. (Bletting is when the fruit is left until bacterial action has caused internal fruit decay — not visible from the outside.) This tree is very long-lived.

S. aucuparia, the Mountain Ash or Rowan, is a very hardy species from Zone 2 and is to be found over almost the whole of Europe and in western Asia, sometimes at high altitudes in conditions where few other trees survive. In a sheltered place it can grow to 50–60 ft (15–18 m), but often only 15–20 ft (5–6 m) in cultivation. I think it is a great asset to the garden, as although it prefers an acid soil, my two trees have grown and flowered and fruited well on heavy clay ground. The yellowy-grey trunk goes very dark later, with longitudinal cracks; the pinnate leaves are toothed, except at the base of the 9–15 leaflets, turning scarlet or yellow in autumn; the buds are slim, downy and browny-mauve. After flowering in May the green and yellow fruits ripen to a bright red in September. If you can pick them before the birds have taken them all, the berries, high in Vitamin C, make a very pleasant and astringent jelly for the table, and are used, as well, in the making of herbal remedies. This tree is now widely planted in North America, and it is said it was, at one time, always given a place in the gardens of houses in the Scottish Highlands to protect against witchcraft. So I feel well-guarded!

There are some good varieties, notably *S. aucuparia* 'Beissneri' which has a beautiful coppery-coloured trunk and branches. The leaves have a yellowy tinge, especially when young, on rich red petioles, and so deeply lobed or cut as to produce a fern-like effect. *S. aucuparia* 'Fastigiata' is ideal for a small space as its branches grow very erect, so producing a narrow columnar tree, with shining large clusters of deep red berries and large dark green leaves. *S. aucuparia* 'Sheerwater Seedling' is also upright in growth and has masses of attractive orange fruits. Then for the variety that has amber-yellow fruits *S. aucuparia* 'Xanthocarpa' should be planted. *S. aucuparia* 'Pendula' is a small wide-spreading weeping tree.

Sorbus 'Apricot Lady' is a seedling of *S. aucuparia* with large apricot berries and sharply divided bright green leaves, turning a rich colour before falling, the large bunches of berries remaining to decorate the bare branches well into winter.

S. cashmiriana from Kashmir and Zone 4 is a charming small tree, usually not more than 15 ft (5 m), with greeny-grey pinnate leaves of 17–19 toothed leaflets and pale pink blooms in May, followed by large hanging clusters of pure-white berries, nearly ½ in (1.2 cm) across, on pinky stalks. They have the desirable habit of remaining on the tree well into winter, and, as I have mentioned earlier, for some reason are the last to be taken by the birds, and sometimes not at all, so can be enjoyed as a decoration for longer in the garden.

S. hupehensis is another small tree, native to Western China and Zone 5, but often to be seen in European gardens and parks as its moderate height of around 30 ft (10 m) and upright, narrow shape of erect brownish-purple branches, makes it an accommodating tree to grow. It has rounded clusters of whitish flowers in May with purply-pink anthers. The white fruits are touched with pink and the foliage is very attractive, as the pinnate leaves, 8–10 in (20–25 cm) long, turn a brilliant red in autumn, having been a dark greenish-blue earlier. The leaflets, 11–13, are on a grooved red stem, toothed only around their tips. The form *S. hupehensis obtusa* does have truly pink fruits, a very pretty variety. With this species the berries remain on the tree well into winter, making an attractive garden decoration at Christmas time.

S. hybrida 'Gibbsii' grows into a very neat tree with large clusters of cherry-size fruits of a rich crimson, and deeply lobed leaves, dark green above and with a grey down underneath. A very striking tree that is extremely hardy.

Even smaller-growing is *Sorbus* 'Joseph Rock', of unknown origin, but probably from China and growing to about 25 ft (8 m). The bright green leaves, composed of 15–19 leaflets, turn brilliant colours in the autumn of orangey-copper to a reddish-purple, and the berries change from an initial creamy colour to a rich amber and stay on the tree most of the winter, as the birds do not like them as much as the darker colours.

One of the choicest of all rowans is the hybrid *Sorbus × kewensis*, raised at Kew Gardens in England. The branches are bent down under the weight of the large clusters of orangey-red fruits. It is a cross between *S. aucuparia* and a lovely species from North China, *S. pohuashanensis*, and has all the merits of both.

S. meliosmifolia, from western China, produces a fascinating brownish berry, having flowered earlier than the other rowans, in April. The purple-brown branches grow erectly, making a neat upright small tree with rich green leaves 7 in (18 cm) long, oval and pointed, and with deeply indented veins. A rather unusual but very decorative tree for the garden, with large simple leaves, totally unlike most of the other species.

S. vilmorinii, from western China and Zone 5, is particularly suitable for very small gardens, growing 15–20 ft (5–6 m) with graceful arched branches of dainty grey-green fern-like leaves which turn red and purple in autumn. The small white flowers become attractive shiny red fruits which fade to pink and nearly white. Because of their colour they also remain on the tree to brighten the dark months for so much longer than those of the quickly eaten red and orange-berried species.

Propagation of the sorbus tree in February is very easy because of the mass of seed produced, but these can take two years to germinate. The hybrids need to be grafted. The only pruning needed is the thinning out of the heads of the trees, if they become too thickly branched.

STEWARTIA

Stewartias are a small genus of about eight to ten trees and shrubs allied to the camellias, so needing an acid soil; but unlike camellias they are deciduous, the oval pointed green leaves turning brilliant colours of purplish-red and chrome-yellow before falling. About half the species become small trees, the one most grown being *S. pseudocamellia* from Japan which makes a delightful

8–15 ft (2.5–5 m) tree, suitable for a half-shaded position, as in an open woodland site.

The flowers are very beautiful, usually a cup of white with a bright yellow boss of stamens in the centre. But *S. virginica* from Maryland in North America has creamy flowers with red stamens. The blooms are over 2½ in (6 cm) across and rather like a single rose. *S. serrata* from Japan has white flowers with a crimson mark on the outside of the petals at the base, and yellow anthers. Its leaves are thicker in texture than the other species, on flattened boughs, with the bark an attractive cinnamon colour. But a very choice stewartia is *S. sinensis* from China, the 2 in (5 cm) cup-shaped flowers being fragrant, a desirable attribute; the elliptical serrated leaves eventually turn a lovely crimson.

Stewartias are quite hardy, tolerating Zone 5 as long as they are given the right conditions. Because of their delicate 2–3 in (5–8 cm) flowers it is best to choose a position where the tree is screened from cutting winds. And they should be planted when quite small, as their roots do not like disturbance later on. They also need shade from the sun, though their heads can be in dappled sun — a similar situation to that most enjoyed by the rhododendrons and eucryphias. Their flowering time, from June to August, fills the gap nicely between the majority of the rhododendrons and that of the eucryphias. Like those of the cistus blooms, the flowers are very short-lived, but are produced over a good period.

The earliest to flower in June or July is *S. koreana* and it has flatter blooms and, like *S. pseudocamellia*, produces intriguing flaking bark on older trees.

I planted *S. pseudocamellia* when I first started gardening and it did very well for several years, producing a mass of flowers. But, with my lack of knowledge then, the position I gave it was too sunny, and too exposed to the westerly gales, and the soil had not been sufficiently prepared to lighten and acidise it. Still, one learns the hard way and now if I do not know a plant and its requirements by heart, I spend some time finding out all about it and whether I have got a suitable position, before I get carried away into acquiring it for my garden, so helping to avoid disappointment.

STYRAX

The styrax is related to the halesia and also used to be known as the Snowdrop Tree, but is now referred to by its American common name Snowbell Tree. The blossoms are very like little snowdrops or snowbells hanging along the branches, but whereas in the case of the halesia they are strung along evenly under the stems, like tiny bells, with the styrax the blooms hang in longer-stalked clusters of flowers with a prominent boss of bright yellow stamens.

The styrax are smaller-growing than the halesias, so make a better choice if space is restricted. The species from the south-eastern area of the United States, *S. americana*, is not as showy as the Japanese species or as easy to grow, though it has attractive 3 in (8 cm) long slightly felted leaves and flowers in June and July with narrower petals; and its habit is more shrub-like. *S. japonica*, from China and Japan, grows to 10 ft (3 m) or more but tends to produce very fan-like branches so that the tree often becomes wider than it is tall. The long gleaming ovate leaves are green above and have a greyish tinge to the undersides.

S. obassia makes a better-shaped tree than *S. japonica* should space be limited, as it develops a nicely rounded form. The leaves are a lovely yellow-touched green, almost round, and 8 in (20 cm) across, and felted beneath. It has the added attraction of fragrant flowers, which appear on stalks at the end of the branches, unlike the other species where they hang below them. The bark is also a feature, as that of the previous year peels off in strips.

S. hemsleyana from western and central China is not unlike *S. obassia* and the leaves are of a similar shape, but have less hair on their undersides; and the leaf buds are more prominent and a rich brown. The intense whiteness of the blooms is especially appreciated when they flower in June.

Like the tamarisk they need to be planted in their permanent positions when young, as they resent later disturbance of the roots. They are deciduous and fairly hardy to and including Zone 5, and also require a lime-free soil; the ideal is sandy loam with added leaf-mould, to remind them of their natural habitat in the woodlands of Japan where it is moist and not too hot. So they naturally do best where there is some shade from nearby trees, and prefer a position where the sun only reaches them towards the end of the day. When trees have flowers hanging from below their branches, they need, if possible, to be sited on the top of a slope or bank, so that you can walk below them, and then see the full beauty of the blooms.

To propagate, take cuttings of half-ripened wood in July or August with a heel, or sow seed in February. The styrax trees, particularly *S. japonica* and the Mediterranean species *S. officinalis*, are the source of the aromatic gum 'Storax', a fragrant resin from which an incense is obtained; and rosaries are also made from the seeds.

Pterostyrax is a very small genus, again allied to the styrax and halesias, being of the same family. It is the best choice of the three to plant where there is lime in the ground as it will tolerate any soil as long as it is rich and deep. *P. hispida* with the intriguing name of the Epaulette Tree, has leaves similar to the halesia and very unusual creamy-yellow fragrant blooms of tress-like fringed bells. The fruits which come after them are ribbed, and slenderer in shape than the rounder felty ones of the styrax tree.

SYRINGA

The syringa is composed of a large genus of completely hardy (Zone 4–5) deciduous shrubs with striking panicles of sweetly scented flowers. In the common species, *S. vulgaris*, the Pipe Tree from Eastern Europe, the blooms are mauve, but there is a wide range of cultivars, the flowers both single and double, with colours ranging from white, through to yellow and shades of red to purple.

However, if they are trained to a single trunk these shrubs will attain tree-size. I have the common one growing against the house and when it gets to the upper windows I cut it down ruthlessly to a couple of feet (60 cm) from the ground and it breaks again and bushes out from the sawn-off trunk. The year after it does not produce flowers, but will do so in future, and my tree has now reached 20 ft (6 m) again after five years, blooming in May when, as long as there is no strong wind to blow it away, the nostalgic perfume heralds the beginning of summer. It is a very versatile plant, in that you can shape it to the size and space you want it to take up, especially when you are not sure what size will eventually be most suitable for a particular situation, and bearing in mind its relation to other shrubs. It throws up a lot of suckers which should always be removed. Cut away, too, all the shoots and spindly branches after flowering, unless you want to keep the form bushy and shrub-like. The leaves are a rich smooth green, and a beautiful heart shape.

Another cultivar that has formed a tree with me is the double-flowered *S. vulgaris* 'Charles Joly', but I have to go to the very bottom of the garden to get the heavy scent of its deep purple blooms. But it is a nice surprise to come across it, flowering, as it does, later than the mauve one. Two other cultivars I think would make a nice range of colour in my garden would be *S. vulgaris* 'Madame Lemoine', also later flowering with perfect double creamy buds, opening to pure-white flowers. And a single one, *S. vulgaris* 'Primrose', with lovely soft yellow dainty blooms, which are a little smaller in size than the average varieties.

However, there are two species that grow easily to tree-size. *S. reticulata* from Japan will reach 30 ft (10 m), with pyramidal-shaped blooms of a rich cream — unfortunately with no scent but they are 10 in long and 6 in wide (25 × 15 cm). The leaves are broad and even more deeply veined than the common variety and downy underneath. *S. pekinensis* from China has looser panicles than *S. reticulata*, and much more tapering leaves and it makes a very graceful tree. They both flower at the end of June. A particularly elegant form is the weeping *S. pekinensis* 'Pendula', quite a sight when the creamy-white blooms drape from the hanging branches. Sometimes the large flower-buds can be damaged by a sharp spring frost, but they are used to colder and longer winters than we have in England and actually do better under these conditions. These last two species have differently shaped flowers to the common lilacs where the stamens are enclosed: in this case the stamens extend beyond the corolla.

The lilacs are happy in any rich soil, and like to be well-mulched. They will grow well on lime, and especially well on chalk.

Many of the cultivars are grafted at the nurseries, but some of the species can be propagated by layering in May, or by cuttings in July.

Though the genus only consists of about 30 species, there are believed to be around 500 cultivars of the common *S. vulgaris*, with a great range of colours and all with the same heady perfume.

TAMARIX

The tamarisks make graceful and delicate foils to the more solid and firmer tree outlines in the rest of the garden scene. They will grow in acid to neutral soil, but prefer a sandy one, so they always do well, and are to be seen planted by the sea, unaffected by salt spray. But they also thrive inland in a sunny, moist, but well-drained situation. Their branches are slender, wreathed in bright green plumate foliage. They look fragile, but are extremely tough, tolerating almost arctic conditions. The flowers are shades of pink — though sometimes almost white — in large sprays of tiny blooms with four or five petals.

T. gallica is the common species used as wind-breaks along the coast, and growing wild in many areas. It is evergreen and comes from the Mediterranean region though is sometimes found as far east from there as India. It flowers from August to October, from shoots of the same year, the bright pink blooms in 1½ in (4 cm) racemes, set against the sharp green foliage and dark brown stems. They all tend to branch profusely from the base.

Flowering about the same time is *T. pentandra*, also from the Mediterranean, much stronger and usually taller-growing — as much as 15 ft (5 m) — with deeper pink flowers produced in a frothy mass from shoots of the current year. The leaves are a richer colour, with a blue-green bloom to them, and the branches a slightly different shade of mauvy-brown. These flowers are scented, and the species *T. pentandra* 'Rubra' has even deeper pink blooms, and is, perhaps, the choicest of all.

The species *T. tetrandra* is the earliest to flower, in May or June, and produces shorter spikes of pale pink racemes from long slim sprays of branches, before the appearance of the leaves. Always prune the tamarisks every year or they will soon get very leggy and straggly.

T. tetrandra purpurea, also known as *T. parviflora*, has deeper pink flowers than the type and slightly different colour branches, and minute leaves. Because of the time they bloom the two varieties of *T. tetrandra* must be pruned immediately after flowering, because they bloom on the previous year's growth, whereas the later-flowering species bloom on the current year's shoots, and should be pruned at the end of February.

From a genus of about 100 species, in the half-dozen of the best-known ones, the variation in colour of flower, leaf and branch is apparent, but there is not much to choose between them; they are all delightfully feathery and give quite an unusual effect in the garden. The best time to propagate them is by taking cuttings in October and placing these straightaway in the position you want the new tree to grow, as they do not move well because of a very long tap root.

TILIA

The tilia, known commonly as the Lime or Linden, consists of a genus of around 50 species of deciduous and very ornamental trees, confined to the North Temperate Zone but not North-West America. Perhaps they are most loved for the scented, creamy-white flowers which fill the air with fragrance on a still day in summer, particularly noticeable when they line avenues and drives. Many of the species attract bees, though some of these, like *T. petiolaris*, are, unfortunately, narcotic to them. Aphids are also attracted to some of the limes and the sticky mess of honeydew that drops on the ground below these trees can be a bit of a menace.

The Common Lime or European Linden, *T.* × *europaea* and hardy in Zone 3, used to be the one most often seen lining the streets, and is the tallest of the

British broad-leaves. But it has two drawbacks in that it is one of those attractive to aphids, making the pavements below dangerously tacky, and its tendency to sucker profusely is also a disadvantage. The oval to heart-shaped bright green leaves are toothed and hairless except for a few downy tufts on the veins underneath. The small pendulous clusters of yellowy-white flowers are a source of nectar for bees, and the dried blossoms make a delicious tea. It grows eventually to around 120 ft (35 m) and so makes an ideal tree in a large park or garden where it can have plenty of space around it. The scented flowers come in early July in drooping clusters of 4–10. The following fruits are ⅓ in (0.8 cm) long and downy. The cultivar *T. × europaea* 'Wratislaviensis' is worth growing, where there is room, for its attractive colouring, the leaves being chrome-yellow at first and changing to green as they mature.

T. cordata, the Small-leaved Lime of Zone 3, from the Caucasus, Siberia and Europe and also native to the British Isles, does not grow so tall as the Common Lime but is still rather large for the average garden. The sweetly scented small ivory flowers come in late July after some of the other limes have flowered, in spreading clusters of 5–10 blooms, followed by thin-shelled, round felty fruits. The leaves are smaller than most limes, around 2 in (5 cm) long, toothed, and a very attractive heart shape and a shiny tough dark green, paler underneath with a blue-white patina. The bark is grey and smooth when young, changing to a darker colour and cracking with age, the trunk being short and thick. The form *T. cordata* 'Swedish Upright' is very useful in certain aspects as its ascending branches give it a narrow columnar shape and although tall, it is not very wide, so does not occupy much horizontal space.

T. americana, the American Lime, American Linden or Basswood, comes from Central and Eastern North America and South-East Canada and Zone 2. It will reach 70 ft (20 m) in the wild, but not so great a height as the previous two species. The coarsely toothed leaves are large, about 8 in long and 15 in wide (20 × 38 cm) and a light green. The group of yellowish-white flowers open in early July and the fruits are tiny, quite smooth like a nut. Unfortunately, it is said that, like the American Beech, this species does not flourish in the British Isles and Europe, perhaps because it cannot tolerate air pollution. This is a great loss as the enormous leaves make it a very handsome tree, and especially as it is such a valuable source of nectar for honey bees in North America; though it does suffer from the attention of aphids. *T. americana* 'Redmond' is recommended as a good form because of its dense conical habit.

T. × euchlora, the Crimean Linden, is a very attractive hybrid between *T. cordata*, the Small-leaved Lime, and a rather rare species from Southern Europe and Iran, *T. dasystyla*. It is a little tenderer, from Zone 5, but makes a beautiful shape with its pendulous branches hanging with large and long-stalked glossy dark green leaves. The flowers in groups of 3–7 appear in late July and are a brighter yellow and larger than other limes, but sadly, though attractive to bees, have a narcotic effect on them, and the poor creatures can be seen lying on the ground beneath the branches. However, this tree is not attractive to aphids, so avoids the sticky sap exudations of some of the other limes. The fruits are downy and elliptic.

T. mongolica, the Mongolian Lime from Northern China and Mongolia and Zone 3, is the ideal lime to plant in a small garden as it forms a neat rounded shape and has small leaves about 2 in (5 cm) long, deeply cut and with toothed edges. Its attractive feature is that the shiny green leaves become a bright yellow in autumn. In fact, this tree is very unlike the other limes, the leaves looking rather similar to those of the thorn or ivy.

T. tomentosa, the Silver Lime or Silver Linden from South-Eastern Europe and South-West Asia and Zone 4, grows very slim when young because of the erect way the branches develop. It gradually widens as the tips of the branches hang down, the large oval leaves very eye-catching in any wind with their alternating colours of the dark green wrinkled uppers and white felty undersides. The very scented flowers open in late July, followed by five-ridged long downy fruits, but again they are of the kind narcotic to bees.

T. petiolaris, the Weeping Silver Lime or Pendant Silver Linden from Zone 5, is related to *T. tomentosa* with the same attractive but narrower leaves, and scented flowers, also fatally attractive to bees. The ridged fruits, ½ in (1.2 cm) long, are rarely fertile. But it grows into a magnificent weeping tree, perfect as a focal point on a large lawn, the branches sweeping downwards and nearly as spectacular as a willow.

T. platyphyllos the Broad-leaved Lime or Big-leaved Linden, from all over Europe and the British Isles and Zone 3, develops into a very large pyramid-shaped tree like the Common Lime but does not indulge in the latter's suckering habit to anywhere near the same extent — nor suffer so much from disease — and its leaves and twigs are downy. The roundish leaves are very large, up to 5 in (12 cm) wide, the biggest of the European limes. They are very dark green with pale hairy undersides. The strongly scented flowers open in late June followed in October by ridged downy pear-shaped fruits. The dark grey trunk has narrow cracks. The variety *T. platyphyllos* 'Laciniata' makes a much smaller, cone-shaped and dense tree with deeply lobed leaves, the pointed ends forming tails. And *T. platyphyllos* 'Rubra', the Red-twigged Lime, is a very desirable tree for street planting as it doesn't mind polluted air and grows neatly, because of the erect formation of the branches. The heart-shaped leaves are unequal and almost hairless. The bright red twigs make a lovely show of colour, particularly for the winter scene. This species is said to be very long-lived, and the white silky soft wood is popular with wood-carvers.

Propagation is most successful from grafting and layering, for the seeds often prove infertile. You can also use rooted suckers.

The limes are very easy to grow, happy in any good loamy soil, and most of them very hardy, and they can be pruned when necessary with no ill effects. Do this in winter while the sap is quiescent. They prefer to be planted in full sun but will stand some shade. There is a fine example of a pleached lime walk enclosing the Sunken Garden at Kensington Gardens in London.

TRACHYCARPUS

The palm family consists of over 2,000 species and most of them grow in tropical and sub-tropical climates. But the small genus *Trachycarpus* can survive in temperate conditions and one of the hardiest (Zone 6/7) is the Windmill Palm, *T. fortunei* (*Chamaerops excelsa*), also known as the Chusan Palm. It was given this name by Robert Fortune because he found it growing freely on the island of Chusan, off the coast of China, south of Shanghai. But it also grows in all other temperate areas of the Far East. It was a great favourite in Victorian times and is seen in many parts of the South and West of England and Eire. Some trees have now reached a great age and height, several in Dorset and in Cornwall being over 40 ft (12 m). And it is a great favourite in many areas of the Mediterranean, too.

The trunk is covered with a mat of fibres, used in rope-making; the palmate leaves coming from the top of the trunk, which is always single. They are like divided fans 2 ft (60 cm) long and 3 ft (1 m) across, dark green above with a waxy bloom underneath. As the lower hands of leaves die and become bedraggled and brown, they can be cut off where the fiercely toothed stalks join the stem and gradually a thick trunk develops covered with this mat of coarse fibres consisting of the remains of the old leaf bases. There are unisexual flowers on the same tree and these appear in early summer, from beneath the fresh green sprays of leaves at the top and hang down around the fibrous trunk. They consist of clusters of tiny fragrant yellow flowers, in panicles up to 2 ft (60 cm) long, which last for quite a long time till the kidney-shaped or circular purple-blue fruits finally appear.

This palm is very frost hardy; some shelter helps to protect the huge leaves from strong winds but my two trees have come through very severe winters unharmed, and one of the trees, growing in a more favourable site, has reached 12 ft (4 m) and is well above the garden fence and open to the westerly gales, yet seems unaffected by them.

I brought these two as little suckers, 6 in (15 cm) high, back from my sister's garden in Devon about 25 years ago and they give an attractively exotic air to the garden. When sitting near them I find the special sound the leaves make, as the air rustles the huge fans, very soothing. But this palm can, also, be easily grown from seed. When the plants are very small they are slightly tender, so surrounding bushes help to protect them; or they can be raised in tubs in a greenhouse, and then hardened off. But once they have established themselves, they will tolerate extreme cold, as long as their heads are in the sun.

They like to be planted in a rich well-drained soil and benefit from a top-dressing of manure from time to time. But they are very suitable for a small space as they grow very slowly, and being evergreen are a pictorial asset to the garden all the year round.

ULMUS

The Elm, ulmus, is a genus of some 45 species that like a deep moist soil and although the dread Dutch Elm disease has decimated the countryside, it is to be hoped that most of the stricken trees will be replaced in time. The disease was first seen in Holland in 1919, hence its name, and was discovered in England not far from London in 1927 and gradually became more and more prevalent with disastrous results. Now the pattern and look of the countryside in Great

Britain, and wherever else it has struck, has been changed irrevocably by the loss of these noble trees. Of course, most of them are far too large and spreading for an ordinary garden and, in fact, *U. procera* the English Elm should never be planted near other trees and shrubs or near buildings as its roots produce suckers and are far-reaching and very disrupting. Another hazard is that when the tree gets old a large branch may suddenly fall with no warning. So strictly a loner to be admired from afar, where plenty of space is available. They do tend to grow in some isolation and not in groups. The English Elms, at one time wild in Southern England and such a picture of flaming leaves in the autumn, and particularly affected by the disease, were often seen in hedges by the roadside as they withstood cold winds and acted as a good wind-break against salt-laden gales.

Though not comparable in size or appearance, there are some elms which are not affected by this crippling disease that has so afflicted most of them. And they grow to a more reasonable height, suitable for planting in an average garden. The safest of these to grow would be *U. parvifolia*, the Chinese Elm, with smaller leaves than the grand elms but still with the characteristic uneven, lop-sided appearance and toothed edge to their oval pointed shape. And the form called *U. parvifolia* 'Frosty' might be even better where there is lack of space, as it is very slow in growth and barely reaches tree-size. Another slightly taller-growing species, the Siberian or Dwarf Elm *U. pumila*, which will grow in Zone 4, one lower than *U. parvifolia*, has again small, but narrow and paler green leaves; and a very desirable variety, *U. pumila arborea*, would make a nice specimen some distance from the house and centred, perhaps, as a feature on a lawn.

The English Elm could be a wonderful sight with its little bunches of red flowers along the bare branches in spring; though its seeds are not fertile and the tree reproduces from suckers. With *U. parvifolia* the flowers appear in autumn, a pale green among the darker shiny leaves, which, with this species particularly, remain on the tree well into winter.

A very elegant weeping form of *U. glabra*, the Wych Elm or Scotch Elm, which has some risk of disease, is *U. glabra* 'Camperdownii'. This is a far more compact and neater-growing form than 'Pendula', making a pretty dome shape of dark green leaves, and these, though larger than those of the previous species, stand up very well to chill winds and coastal exposure. The spring flowers appear before the leaves and are again pale green, but the winged seed-heads which follow attractively string the branches.

Great efforts are being made to replace the lost elms and I know of one nursery where they are able to supply 7–8-year-old trees for instant planting, or a 1-year-old 'whip' (a long twig or slender branch) as a start off — for less ambitious planters.

VIBURNUM

Most of the viburnums are really shrub-like in form, but I think three varieties make a good showing as trees for the average garden. *V. opulus* 'Sterile', often called the Snowball tree or Guelder Rose, has quite large balls of white flower-heads in June and by autumn there are bright red berries. Then the three-lobed and toothed leaves also turn scarlet, but are matt, whereas the berries are bright and shining, and these remain after the leaves have fallen. It is widespread in parts of Europe and Asia and in North Africa, and grows very happily in damp situations, in fact it is sometimes called the Water Elder. There was a very elegant tree in a garden near me, which had grown to 15 ft (5 m) or more and was quite a feature when in flower, covered with the pure-white snowballs; but alas someone hacked it down to 'tidy' the garden and I miss the sight of this tree with its blooms glistening in the sun of a May or June morning.

The two other viburnums are evergreen; the Laurustinus, *V. tinus*, is common enough, but I have found it extremely good value in the garden, particularly as it is happy near the sea. In some years I have pruned the plants heavily, which they do not resent, and after a year of leaf, come into a dome of flower again. But with two of my viburnums I have not pruned them and they have grown into handsome trees, sometimes with additional branches, but one particularly making a solid dome of shiny green leaves all the year above a single trunk, and during the winter months the florets of white blooms mass on the branches, with their sweet delicate scent, on a tree now 20 ft (6 m) high. It always makes quite a feature in the garden — a back-cloth of flowers all winter and cool dark green foliage all summer long.

The other evergreen makes a very handsome shrub and eventually attains tree-size, as it has in my garden after many years. *V. rhytidophyllum* has very luxuriant deeply indented large leaves and produces in May heads of creamy-white flowers. But it is the leaves which give it such an exotic appearance.

All these viburnums grow happily on any soil, particularly on chalk; and another one native to Europe, the Wayfaring Tree, *V. lantana*, can be found growing on downland, to 15 ft (5 m) high and as much across with its May-flowering white blooms and oblong autumn fruits, first bright red then turning black as the leaves become dark red. Quite effective but perhaps too straggly in growth to try in the average garden.

The viburnums are very tough and most will survive in Zone 3, *V. tinus* being not quite so hardy, but standing up well to prolonged frost.

WISTERIA

The wisteria, which is sometimes spelt wistaria in older plant books, is usually thought of as a deciduous wall plant or climber, but it can be trained very successfully as a standard tree. When grown against a house it soon climbs to the roof and can damage the tiles and gutters with its persistent twining shoots and becomes very difficult to control and to prune.

I decided to plant the Chinese Wisteria, *W. sinensis*, as a free-standing tree which could be admired from the house and yet sited with other trees and shrubs to the windward side of it for protection. When very young it commenced flowering and has formed a nice weeping head. The side growths are shortened each year to produce flowers and eventually when the tree has reached the height required, these side shoots will be removed. They are left on when the tree is young, to feed the roots and encourage growth. *W. sinensis* has mauve pea flowers in 8–12 in (20–30 cm) racemes, opening together and very fragrant in warm weather. There are varieties that are white, a double purple and double lilac, but the mauve of my tree coming in May, framed by the pinnate fronds of fresh green leaflets, which have silky hairs at first, makes a lovely complement to the darkness of the flower that follows from June to September as the *Clematis* 'Niobe' I have planted to grow up the trunk carries its dark ruby-red blooms. In this way I have flower colour in this small space from May to September. The 6 in (15 cm) long tapering silvery-green velvety seed pods are a further decoration later on in the season.

The Japanese Wisteria, *W. floribunda*, does not grow so tall as the Chinese species and curiously the stems twine in a clockwise direction whereas the Chinese one travels anti-clockwise, so you can always tell which plant you are looking at; and it flowers later than *W. sinensis*, with the blooms more widely spaced on the racemes. There are also colour variations in *W. japonica*, with double and single flowers, including pink, and one, *W. floribunda* 'Macrobotrys', has enormous pale lavender racemes which can be 3–4 ft (1–1.2 m) long. But this variety needs the support of a pergola to hold up the fantastic blooms, and would be too fragile alone as a tree specimen.

It is wisest to go to a good supplier for your wisteria, as the better-grafted tree plants grown in containers will then flower very early as mine did, and soon add an unusual and elegant tree to the garden scene.

The site needs to be in full sun and the soil well-enriched to begin with; they grow slowly for the first few years.

Propagation can be done in late spring by layering stems in May, or by taking cuttings in August.

ZELKOVA

Zelkova is of the same family as the elms, and consists of a small deciduous genus, only five species being cultivated. It differs from the elm in that it has male and female flowers separate, but on the same tree, and single not double toothing around the edge of the leaves.

Z. carpinifolia (crenata) hails from the Caucasian mountains and is one of the strangest and most unique shapes in the world of trees, and very long lived. It has a short trunk, grey and smooth like a beech — whereas that of the elm is uneven with deep clefts — and this scales off with age, giving an attractive mottled effect. From this stout trunk masses of horizontal branches grow straight up, and in winter make a stunning oval outline against the sky. The elliptical dark green leaves, 1½–3 in (4–8 cm) long, feel rough when handled. This tree will eventually reach 80 ft (25 m), but about one-third of that height in 15–20 years. The tiny green scented flowers open in April with the leaves, which turn a golden-brown before they fall. There is a lovely weeping form, *Z. carpinifolia* 'Pendula', which develops a beautiful shape to have in the garden.

Z. serrata (acuminata), known as the Keaki, is a native of Japan, Korea and China, and is much used in Japan for Bonsai work, and also grown along avenues and rivers there as a shelter belt. The beautiful orangey-brown coloured wood, revealed by the flaking, is much valued in the making of furniture. Its form is more wide-spreading than Z. *carpinifolia*, producing a more rounded shape, with longer, slimmer, 2–5 in (5–12 cm) long, coarsely toothed leaves; and these turn a rich copper at the end of the summer. The small green flowers, very like those of Z. *carpinifolia*, open in May, the females singly at the tip of the shoots, and the males in clusters and a little larger, from the leaf axils at the base of the growths.

On the whole, zelkovas eventually grow to too large a specimen for the small garden, but on a reasonably sized lawn they can give a very dramatic effect. However, Z. *sinica* from China is comparatively smaller-growing and makes an interesting feature in the big garden when the young leaves, shorter — being 1–2 in (2.5–5 cm) long — than the other species but also rough, have a pinkish touch in spring and the bark flakes even more than the others and therefore has a great deal of the elegant orange showing through the peeling grey. And it is reputed to be perfectly hardy.

Z. *verschaffeltii* tends to grow in a wide-spreading shrubby form, but if it is trained to one leading trunk it will make a more upright tree, with graceful deeply lobed leaves and attractive flaking bark.

Z. *cretica* (*abelicea*), found in the mountains of Crete, is very rare, but well worth cultivating as it reaches no more than 45 ft (14 m) in maturity and often remains less than half this height and quite shrub-like and suitable for growing in a garden. The fragrant white flowers appear at the same time as the hairy 1 in (2.5 cm) long crenate dark green, leathery leaves, the slim twigs being downy.

Z. *serrata* will tolerate Zone 5 whereas Z. *carpinifolia* needs it no colder than Zone 6 to do well. It is advisable to give very young trees some protection from frost by screening and mulching. They are easy as to type of soil as long as it is rich, deep and well-drained, and though preferring a sunny position, they will grow well in a certain amount of shade, and are unaffected by atmospheric pollution.

The fruits which develop in autumn are green nuts like a hairy pea. Zelkovas can be grown from seed or they can be grafted by using elm stock.

15 *Magnolia campbellii mollicomata*: Pink Tulip Tree

16 *Clematis montana* growing up a *Prunus cerasifera* 'Pissardii': Purple-leaved Plum Tree

17 *Pyrus salicifolia* 'Pendula': Weeping Willow-leaved Pear

18 *Sorbus aucuparia*: Mountain Ash or Rowan

CHAPTER 2
Selected Trees Grown for Fruit

MALUS

In my fruit garden I try to have trees that give good returns and also to grow unusual fruit, for the ordinary kinds are so plentiful and easy to buy, and where space is restricted, a fig or a morello cherry would be more interesting to have than the ubiquitous apple and pear. Not that these are to be despised. I have inherited two large old bramley apple trees, which are now a good shape and should crop heavily after their judicious pruning two years ago. They had become so tall and spread-out after over 60 years that the apples were impossible to pick, and windfalls have their limits and cannot be stored for winter use, which the bramley fruit does so well, becoming sweet enough to eat by February and March, after the months of quiet ripening.

A year ago I planted my favourite eating apple — over the centuries there have been more than 3,000 named varieties — the *Malus domestica* 'Cox's Orange Pippin', which, with all the wonderful breeds that have been produced recently, is, I think, still incomparable for flavour, crunchiness and attractive colouring. I have planted it against a fence as a cordon as it is not the easiest apple to grow and will not tolerate colder districts, where it must have the shelter of a wall. The 'Cox' needs a well-drained soil and regular potash dressings and pruning. It ripens for picking in October and keeps beautifully through the winter. There is a lovely new 'Cox' being grown organically, which makes it of great interest, to be called 'Pearl'.

My second choice would be *Malus domestica* 'Ashmead's Kernel', a delicious russet, also with a firm texture and excellent flavour and aroma. This is an old variety raised in 1720 in Gloucester, more than a century earlier than the first seedling of 'Cox's Orange Pippin', and although not a good cropper, the flavour is superb.

These two trees can be grown in their natural upright, slightly spreading, form, or as a cordon, bush, fan, espalier, pyramid or dwarf pyramid, and also in spindlebush and standard or half-standard forms, depending on the space you

26 *Malus domestica* 'Cox's Orange Pippin': Desert Apple

27 *Malus* 'John Downie': Crab Apple

have and the shape you wish to grow it — whether against a wall or as a specimen on a lawn or forming a small orchard. They can even be grown in a very large tub on a patio, or bought as miniature trees with the fruit already developing — several can be planted in a neat row along a path on the edge of the vegetable bed — and these tiny ones are called 'step-over' trees.

Most of the other species of the Flowering Crabs from the *Malus* genus are ornamental, vying with the prunus in their spring blossom, from white to pink and deep red, but there are three that have particular value for their lovely white flowers and elegant decorative little fruits. Those of *Malus* 'John Downie', a tree which grows to 20 ft (6 m) and of Zone 4, having pink buds opening to white flowers, then conical and scarlety-orange fruits with the most delicious flavour and pink colour when made into jelly. *M. baccata*, the Siberian Crab is found through East Asia to North China, where it can reach 40–50 ft (12–15 m), and forming a nice rounded shape. It can tolerate Zone 2 and is very resistant to apple diseases. There are very fragrant white flowers in May, and then smaller cherry-like fruits which are a brilliant red, with no trace of a calyx when ripe; these, too, make an excellent jelly. The third crab-apple, which is good for both flowers and fruit, is *Malus* 'Golden Hornet', which grows into a small tree about 20 ft (6 m) and is tolerant of Zone 4. The white flowers are followed by heavy crops of circular bright golden fruits which, if not picked, will persist on the tree far into winter, well after the leaves have fallen. This variety is a good tree to plant in an orchard as it will pollinate any other apple.

PYRUS

There are now over 1,000 cultivated varieties of the garden pear, *Pyrus communis*, that once grew wild over Southern Europe. The timber is much used for furniture making as it has an even grain and a pinkish-brown colour. The fruit is like an apple in some respects but the shape is more elongated, the flesh grittier to the taste and the thicker stalk is not set deep in the fruit. The shiny green leaves are rounded or oval and often turn a rich colour in the autumn. Pears need a very much warmer site than apples, being from Southern Europe; though said to tolerate Zone 4, they fruit more successfully in the southern and western parts of Britain, and must have a sunny aspect and will do best with their backs against a warm wall, where netting can be hung over the branches if the weather is severe. They flower in April and do not like cold northerly or easterly winds which can damage the blossom, and they like a warmer, richer soil than the apple.

There are three varieties I favour, rather different in shape and taste but all happy to be grown as espaliers or cordons. *P. communis* 'Bon Chrétien', also known as the 'Williams' pear, or 'Bartlett' in America, has a lovely musky flavour. The fruit is large and very juicy, a soft pale green, ready to pick during September and it should be gathered when still green. It ripens to a pale yellow, with faint red lines and russet spots. The trouble with this pear is that it is only perfect for a day or so, very quickly turning 'sleepy' and floury and unpleasant to eat. *P. communis* 'Conference' is the most widely grown pear in Britain, raised in Berkshire about 1700. It is resistant to scab, which the 'Williams' pear is not, and very prolific. It is slimmer, with a longer neck and a deep green russeted reddish-brown. It is ready for picking in late September and does not turn colour on ripening, being ready from October to November. Despite its firmer appearance and feel, it is a juicy fruit with a delicious and aromatic flavour. My third choice is *P. communis* 'Doyenné du Comice' with a marvellous flavour and fatter shape than the 'Williams'. It is ready for picking in early October and ripe a week or so after that. It does not keep well like the 'Conference', but with these three varieties you have a pear to eat from September to Christmas. I had a large 20 ft (6 m) tree of 'Doyenné du Comice' which never seemed to set fruit or, when it did, keep it very long. In a particularly warm spring and hot summer 90 pears swelled and ripened on the tree, a feast of delicious eating. But at no other time has the tree repeated this bounty, perhaps because the springs have been too cold, or possibly because a tree that pollinated it in that good year may now have been cut down by nearby builders, and I need to plant a new pollinator to replace it. It is one of the most difficult pears to induce to crop, anyway, but well worth a try for the fantastic results when the conditions are just right. But before planting, it is a good idea to find out from a local nursery what variety does well in your district.

CYDONIA

Cydonia oblonga is the Common Quince and a native of Turkestan and Northern Iran, but grown elsewhere in the Mediterranean, particularly in Portugal and France. It has long been cultivated, and was much valued by the Romans. It is deciduous and perfectly hardy, tolerating Zone 4, but does need strong sun to ripen the fruit well and has a better chance of this if given the added warmth of a wall. But in southern districts it makes an elegant lawn specimen.

The quince is quite a small tree 20–25 ft (6–8 m), sometimes upright with strong branches but often developing a deformed shape as if bent by the wind and the weight of its leaves. These are rounded, oval and dark green, with a very felted underside. They often turn golden-yellow in autumn. The solitary or clustered pink and white flowers, 2 in (5 cm) across, open in May. The fruit is similar to the pear and the apple, but has up to 20 ovules in each central section instead of two. It is pear-shaped, 3–4 in (8–10 cm) long, and often coated with a thick white felt. The fruit ripen to a rich yellow from October onwards, and the scent they give off is sharp and astringent but quite intoxicating. They are very hard to peel and the central core is difficult to remove, but the hard and acid flesh makes the most wonderful jam; and it is also valued as a flavouring to be added when cooking apples and pears. In France the quince is called *coing* and a famous sweetmeat is made in Orléans called 'Cotignac' where the fruit, sometimes with oranges added, are boiled and sieved again and again with sugar to make a firm slab which is cut into squares and stored in jars and often eaten with cream cheese. In Portugal the quince is known by its Spanish name 'Marmelo' from which the original marmalade, which we make with Seville oranges only, was made.

There are several varieties, the ones seen in England are: 'Ispahan', a very strong-growing form found in Iran; 'Meech's Prolific', a very heavy cropper; 'Bereczki', which has beautiful flowers but is not such a good bearer of fruit; 'Champion', which is very fertile but the fruit has not such a good flavour; 'Maliformis', the apple-shaped variety; and the one I think is the choicest, 'Portugal', with large fruits of a delicious scent which make the best jam of a rich dark red. The fruits should be gathered when ripe at the end of October, never when wet, and stored till they have turned yellow. In a cool frost-free place they will then keep for two or three months.

These trees should be planted in early autumn, either as a standard, half-standard or bush. They like a moist soil, and do particularly well when planted near a pond or stream. In addition to being grown for its fruit, the quince is much grown as a rootstock for pears.

MESPILUS

The Medlar *Mespilus germanica*, is a deciduous tree consisting of a genus of a single species but related to the *Crataegus* (hawthorn) and has similar flowers. It comes from Asia Minor and South-East Europe and Zone 5. It has been grown for a long time in England, even naturalising in some areas. But is has not been cultivated a great deal since the eighteenth century. This is a pity because it is a very elegant tree for the garden; either as a 15–20 ft (5–6 m) wide-spreading specimen, sometimes crooked in habit with a very rugged bark; or when grown as a standard, 8–10 ft (2.5–3 m) tall, it makes a good talking point, with single white flowers, like a wild rose and nearly 1½ in (4 cm) across, which open in late May or early June at the end of short young shoots. The distinctive tawny-brown round fruits, 1 in (2.5 cm) across, are curiously open at one end, where the seeds are visible. This tree is hardier than the quince, but in colder countries the fruit does not ripen for eating on the tree as in Italy, but they should be picked before the first frost touches them and left for two or three weeks till they lose their green tint and are almost rotten and soft, known as 'bletted' (bacterial action causing internal fruit decay), when they are surprisingly palatable, and also make a pleasant jam or jelly, if the seeds are removed — an excellent accompaniment to meats and cheeses.

The large, oval to lance-shaped leaves are downy and turn brown-red before falling. The Medlar is particularly free from diseases and pests and will grow in any good well-drained soil. It needs an open, sunny situation, if possible protected from cold winds by giving it the shelter of a wall, especially in northern districts.

There are several varieties, but when choosing bear in mind that the size of the tree is proportionate to that of the fruit. 'Nottingham' or 'Narrow-leaved Dutch' has small to medium pear-shaped, russeted, yellowish-brown fruits, and with 'Royal' the fruit is medium-sized, roundish, reddish-brown. Both of these forms are prolific with excellent flavoured fruit.

Prune by thinning out weak and old wood in winter, and keep the tree open. The fruit is borne on old spurs, at the ends of the branches. The wild tree has thorns, but in cultivation it is thornless except in very old specimens.

28 *Mespilus germanica* 'Nottingham': Medlar

MORUS

Morus is a small genus of about a dozen deciduous trees and shrubs, and the two most commonly grown are the Common Mulberry or Black Mulberry, *Morus nigra*, and the White Mulberry, *Morus alba*.

The White Mulberry is a native of Asia and is grown there and all over Southern Europe, for its light green leaves are the food plant on which the silkworm feeds. Four acres (1.6 ha) of the grounds of Buckingham Palace were once planted with mulberries by James I, who wanted to establish a silk farm. Unfortunately, by mistake, the Black Mulberry was planted, which produced beautiful fruit but was not attractive to the silkworms. The White Mulberry has little white, pink or purple fruits but they are rather insipid. There is a lovely weeping form, *M. alba* 'Pendula', with graceful grey branches or large, heart-shaped leaves forming a canopy of light green foliage which is umbrella-shaped and resembles the weeping form of the Wych Elm, *Ulmus glabra*. In autumn the leaves turn a lovely yellow — they are glossier and less downy than the Common Mulberry.

The Black Mulberry comes from Western Asia, but was established in Europe in ancient times and mentioned by Greek and Roman writers. It forms a very picturesque tree for the garden, and is smaller-growing than the white species, which can attain 30 ft (10 m), with a short rugged trunk below a domed head of crooked branches. The leaves are dark green and unevenly toothed and sometimes lobed, but always heart-shaped at the base, and they can be 3–9 in (8–20 cm) long, the uppers covered with short rough hairs and the lower sides with down. The flowers are in separate catkins, males about 1 in (2.5 cm) long and the females barely ½ in (1.2 cm), similar to those of the White Mulberry. But the raspberry-like fruit grows to 1 in (2.5 cm) long, twice the size of the white kind, and ripens to a delicious purple-black which stains the hands and lips when they are eaten. Because they have to be picked when fully ripe, they are not grown much commercially, as the fruit is then squashy and is best picked and eaten straight from the tree. A cloth spread under the tree will catch the ripe fruit if the tree is shaken. It can sometimes be so heavily laden with fruit that the branches must be supported to stop them breaking off. The most delicious wine or jam can be made from these nearly black berries.

The mulberries like a deep rich well-drained soil and do well in town or seaside gardens. Their roots are fleshy and brittle so plant them with care in October-November or February-March and do not shorten the long roots, as is usual when planting fruit trees, or they will 'bleed' and the tree may die. The White Mulberry is hardier and will tolerate Zone 4 but the Black Mulberry needs Zone 6 and will grow in the open in the south as a specimen tree, bush or standard; but in northern districts it should be given the protection of a warm south wall.

When pruning, as the fruit is borne on spurs and on short-jointed young wood, cut back young shoots to four or five buds. In winter thin overcrowded branches to keep the tree a good shape. When grown against a wall, train the main branches about 15 in (38 cm) apart and allow them to grow till they have covered the wall; side shoots should be cut back in July to five or six leaves, for mulberries grow slowly, particularly *Morus nigra*, which also lives to a great age.

These trees are easily propagated by cuttings of young wood, as much as 3–5 ft (1–1.5 m) long, placed in sandy soil in a cold frame in September or October. Layers also root readily if put down in October, but do not be tempted to use a sucker from around the base of a *Morus nigra* tree, because this may have been grafted on *Morus alba* and you will have something with which to feed silkworms, but not the crop of delicious sweet-sour fruit you are expecting.

The mulberry is practically immune from disease and pests, only the birds being troublesome, for they devour the fruit.

DIOSPYROS

Diospyros is composed of a large genus of both evergreen and deciduous trees and shrubs, most of which need a warm soil and plenty of hot sun to ripen the delicious fruit. The male and female flowers come on separate plants.

D. lotus, the Date Plum, is deciduous and native to China, but cultivated for its fruit in the Far East and Italy and for its ornamental value. The leaves are oval, without teeth, and a glossy dark green paler underneath and 3–5 in (8–12 cm) long. It is quite a small tree, rarely growing more than 30 ft (10 m), though much taller in very warm climates. The flowers are insignificant and appear in July, the males in clusters in the leaf axils and the females similar, but singly and on a separate tree. The fruit are little round balls less than 1 in (2.5 cm) wide, ripening yellow or purple. Though the tree is perfectly hardy, the fruit will not ripen in England.

D. virginiana, the North American Persimmon or Common Persimmon, makes a fine deciduous tree, wide-spreading with pendulous branches, and a dramatic bark very dark and thick, and deeply indented as if cut in rectangular blocks. It is native to the Central and Eastern United States and Zone 4 and will fruit as far north as the Great Lakes. It can grow to 40–65 ft (12–19 m), occasionally much taller and likes a rich well-drained soil. The leaves are much smaller than *D. lotus*, but with the same gloss and dark green colour, turning nice shades in the autumn. The pale yellow flowers are also larger and the fruit a similar shape but twice the size, yellow then a soft pale orange often with a reddish flush on one side, and edible after frost, when they become soft and sweet. It is not often cultivated, but large numbers of the pleasantly astringent fruit are picked from wild trees.

I remember so vividly the first time I came across *D. kaki*, the deciduous Chinese Persimmon tree, in the South of France, covered with its beautiful orange glossy fruits. It is much grown in this region and makes a fine tree to 40 ft (12 m); it is very easy as to soil and can tolerate dry conditions. The large, long oval leaves, again shiny green but downy underneath, turn gorgeous shades of yellow, orange, red and purple in autumn; and that is its chief value in England as it needs Zone 7 and the fruit rarely ripens here unless the tree is given the warmth of a south wall and plenty of sun. These are nearly 3 in (8 cm) in diameter and can be eaten fresh or cooked, and sometimes they are candied. In the South-Eastern United States the trees are usually planted in private gardens, but in California there is a small commercial acreage. In Japan the *D. kaki* is known as Kakee.

Propagation can be by seed, but *D. kaki* is often grafted on to *D. virginiana* to keep its qualities unchanged. These trees need little pruning, the main requirement being to train a good lead.

FICUS

Ficus, the fig, is a genus of over 600 species, belonging to the Mulberry family, but most of them are not suitable for growing in Great Britain.

However, *Ficus carica*, the deciduous Common Fig, is hardy to Zone 6, and native to Western Asia and the Eastern Mediterranean. It is grown all over Southern Europe and in California for its delicious sweet pear-shaped fruits which are eaten raw, dried, tinned or sugared. The figs will ripen in Southern England and as far north as New York in the Eastern United States. The tree grows to 30 ft (10 m) but is often smaller and rather bushy in shape, with a smooth grey trunk. The large palmate shiny dark green leaves have deep 3–5 lobes, rough on the upper surfaces and fine velvety hairs underneath. Males and female flowers come on separate trees and are very strange in that they form inside the tiny fig which swells and develops into a juicy pippy fruit, the skin brown, green or mauve. In warm climates where there is an abundance of sun, or if grown in a greenhouse, they will crop several times a year, but in cooler areas only the spring-formed fruits, which have been embryo fruitlets all winter, mature and ripen by late summer.

The variety usually grown is *F. carica* 'Brown Turkey', and I have a tree, 15 ft high, which is in a very sunny corner of the garden, flanked on one side by a 6 ft (2 m) fence and on the other by the wooden walls of an old potting shed. When I planted it I put rubble in the hole and bricked in the roots well, for if figs are given a lush plentiful soil they will make a mass of gorgeous foliage, but produce little fruit. In a fine warm summer my tree gives a good crop of fruit. Figs do not ripen after picking so they must be left till soft and then gathered quickly before the birds, ants and wasps get at them.

A prolific early-fruiting variety is *F. carica*, 'White Marseilles' with large pale yellowish-green figs of an excellent flavour. There are some centuries-old famous trees on the old library wall of Lambeth Palace in London. But it will grow well in a pot and can be forced early when grown in a greenhouse. *F. carica* 'St. John's' is also a large fig, with white flesh, bearing the fruit early and this, too, is an excellent variety for pot growing. A mid-season fruiting variety is *F. carica* 'Brunswick' with very large brownish red-purple fruits of excellent flavour, and this fig does particularly well out of doors. Then for late-fruiting, choose *F. carica* 'Bourjasotte Grise' with medium to large figs, sweet and rich and a reddish-brown in colour. But this variety must be given a very warm site, either in the greenhouse or in a pot in a very sunny protected corner of the garden. All figs need plenty of sun to ripen the wood.

Propagation is by division of suckers, or cuttings taken of semi-ripe one-year-old wood, 4–6 in (10–15 cm) long, and put in pots in September, or 10–12 in (25–30 cm) cuttings of firm woody shoots inserted against a sheltered wall in autumn.

Pollination with most of the other species is by the female fig wasp, which gets into the flower by entering a small hole at the end of the fig. But the fig wasp does not occur in Britain and the varieties of fig grown here, fortunately, set without pollination.

29 *Ficus carica*: Common Fig

PRUNUS

Apricot   Some of the most delectable fruits come under the species of prunus. *P. armeniaca*, the deciduous Apricot from Central Asia and China and Zone 5, but grown commercially for its fruit crop all over Southern Europe, North Africa and California, forms a sturdy round-headed tree, 20–30 ft (6–10 m) high, the stout trunk having a reddish-brown bark. The flowers come very early in March before the glossy-green broad, long-stalked leaves appear. The young leaves and twigs are tinged with red. The blooms are usually white, or in some varieties they are red in bud, opening to pale pink, and it is a good idea to protect them from late frosts by draping the branches where possible with a light covering such as muslin or polythene. This is simple to do when the apricot is grown and fan-trained against a wall. The fruit varies in colour from pale yellow to deep orange with a red freckled velvety skin, and there are apricots of different flavour, tenderness and size. Unlike a peach the stone inside an apricot easily separates from the flesh. It is self-fertile so a single tree will bear a crop.

A good variety is *P. armeniaca* 'Flore Pleno' with semi-double flowers in March or April. And some excellent cultivars are 'New Large Early' with ripe fruits in mid-July; 'Alfred' and 'Farmingdale', fruiting July to August and both less liable to die-back than other varieties; and 'Moorpark' the most often grown tree and very reliable, fruiting at the end of August to September.

Apricots grow well in soils with a high water table, which have a tendency to be slightly limy, yet well-drained. They will grow out of doors in Great Britain as far north as Ayrshire in Scotland; they need plenty of sun for good fruit production, so a wall sheltered from early morning spring sun, but affording plenty of hot sun later to ripen the fruits, is ideal.

Propagation is by seed, or more usually the apricot is grafted on to plum rootstocks, the usual one being 'St. Julien A' which gives a not too vigorous tree about 15–20 ft (5–6 m) high. An oil is extracted from the seed of the apricot and used in the making of soap and perfumes. The fruit must be left on the tree till ripe and picked dry.

Peaches and Nectarines   The Peach, *P. persica*, is hardier than the apricot, tolerating Zone 4, though still requiring great summer heat to ripen the wood and the fruit: it grows into a bushy willowy tree up to 20 ft (6 m). The peach originated in China, but has been grown all over the world for many centuries. It reached ancient Greece and Rome from Persia — hence its name, because for a long time it was thought to have originated there.

Unlike the apricot the leaves are lanceolate and finely toothed, and the flowers blossom in April with the leaves, later than the apricot, and are a lovely pink, though occasionally white, and larger, up to 1½ in (4 cm) across. The fruit can be 3 in (8 cm) wide, and the flesh usually yellow, though sometimes white or pale green. The white-fleshed is considered to have the best flavour and to be the hardiest in a cold climate. Peaches are round and juicy with a soft velvety skin, so need careful handling to avoid damage. They are tested for ripeness on the tree by feeling near the stalk at the base, never touching the sides of the fruit. They have an exotic scent as they ripen. The stone is deeply furrowed and adheres to the flesh.

Good peach varieties are 'Duke of York', bright crimson with white flesh in mid-July; 'Peregrine', bright scarlet in early August; 'Royal George', large fruit, pale and speckled in late August; and two fruiting in mid-September, 'Barrington' with large yellowish-green peaches marbled red; and 'Bellegarde' also large, and dark crimson. All these have an excellent flavour and will grow well on south walls in the open.

I have a 'Peregrine' peach in my greenhouse, fan-trained on the brick wall of the garage against which the greenhouse is built, and this fruits very well. As I do not like to use any chemical sprays of any kind in my garden, when the peach is attacked by red spider I put in a tiny creature, the predatory mite, *Phytoseiulus persimilis*, which devours the red spider and clears up the trouble very quickly.

The Nectarine is similar to the Peach but has smaller, smooth-skinned fruit with a more delicate flavour, and brighter colour. Some good varieties are 'Early Rivers' which gives an excellent bright red crop in July; 'Lord Napier', fruiting in early August, pale green with a red cheek; and 'Humboldt' which has orange and crimson fruits in August and September. But 'Pine Apple' has about the finest flavour and large orange and red fruits in September.

Nectarines and peaches like a slightly acid soil and a rich, well-drained mixture of compost and peat or well-rotted manure. When planting against a wall — which nectarines prefer, as they need even greater warmth than peaches — make the hole about 8 in (20 cm) away from the bricks, and slope the stem towards the wall. Then mulch well around the roots, but not near the trunk. Always keep well watered, particularly when grown against a wall, until the fruit is ripening. Because of their need of warmth and sun they are normally better fan-trained, so that they can be given extra protection when needed — from a late frost or bird damage; though some bush peaches will do well in a protected garden in Southern England, growing and fruiting successfully, too, in standard and half-standard forms.

Plant between November and March, the autumn being preferable as the trees start in growth very early in the spring.

Propagation can be by seed, but seedling trees do not come true to type and take 5–7 years before they produce fruit, so grafting is more satisfactory, either on 'St. Julien A', or for a more vigorous tree on 'Brompton'.

Cherries   There are two kinds of cherries used for cooking and eating, *Prunus avium*, the Sweet Cherry derived from the Mazzard, Gean or Wild Cherry, from Europe and Western Asia and Eastern North America; the Acid Cherry, *P. cerasus*, or Sour Cherry from South-West Asia, both deciduous and tolerating Zone 3. The Duke Cherry or Royal Cherry is a cross between the two, with an acid/sweet flavour, the best cultivar of this being 'May Duke', fruiting in early to mid-July.

Unfortunately the sweet cherry, and the cross, become far too large for the average garden unless they are grown on 'Colt' stocks, which produces a tree around 30–40 ft (10–12 m), not the 60–70 ft (18–20 m) of its normal growth.

30 *Prunus cerasus*: Sour Cherry

This can make an ideal fan-trained tree and is also a good way to grow the best progeny of the acid cherry, the Morello Cherry, which only makes a small tree and is a good size for the garden, with its drooping branchlets. It is particularly valuable as it will thrive on a north wall, fruiting later there than in other positions, where the cherries ripen in August or September. The Morello is a useful acid cherry as it is self-fertile, and the only sweet cherry to be self-fertile is the cultivar 'Stella', with mahogany-red fruits in late July. With other cultivars another tree, a compatible but different cultivar, is necessary for pollination.

The Morello Cherry bears a heavy crop of dark red fruit, which should be picked with scissors, cutting through the stalks, as pulling them off may damage the bark and cause fungal infection. They are too sharp to eat raw but make the most delicious pies, jam and wine, and are also used for liqueurs and brandy in regions where the trees are found growing wild all over Europe and in their native habitat. For the Sour Cherry is more adaptable to any soil and more resistant to frost damage than the Sweet Cherry, growing at altitudes of up to 6,000 ft (1,830 m). It has thick clusters of white flowers in April or May and the leaves are a glossy green, oval and pointed, with double-toothed edges. *P. cerasus* 'Rhexii' is a lovely double-flowered form, with blooms 1–1½ in (2.5–4 cm) across, and which has been cultivated in England for many centuries.

P. serotina, a species in the Bird Cherry *P. padus* section, is grown in Eastern North America, East and South Mexico and Guatemala. It is a very large tree growing to 100 ft (30 m), with white flowers in racemes in May. The shiny leaves turn yellow in autumn and the fruit, which is said to equal the Morello Cherry, is used for flavouring rum or brandy, and ripens in September. The bark is strongly aromatic and used for furniture, and also grown in Central Europe for its timber, as are the other cherries.

But for the garden, the best-flavoured cultivars of sweet cherries are 'Early Rivers', with black fruit, ready mid- to late June; 'Waterloo', a mid-season black in late June to early July; 'Napoleon Bigarreau', which has very large heart-shaped bright red fruit with white flesh, and is ready in late July; or 'Amber Heart' (Kentish Bigarreau), with pale yellow skin, a red cheek and white flesh. This is a prolific variety and was a great favourite at one time with growers in Kent, a county famous for the cultivation of its cherry orchards.

A very choice white-fleshed cherry is 'Merton Glory', ripe in mid-July; and two recommended new cultivars, more resistant to disease than some of the others, are 'Mermat' with early fruiting black cherries and 'Merchant', also a black cherry but ready a little later, in mid-season, the latter being the best flavoured.

The scented white flowers of *P. avium* come in late April, 1 in (2.5 cm) across, and are cup-shaped and grow in umbels on a long stalk. The leaves are lanceolate and toothed, a little rough on top and hairy beneath; they turn yellow and red in autumn. The bark is smooth and grey at first, becoming russet-red and marked with horizontal lines and large fissures.

When growing a cherry tree as a specimen in a garden, tie the branches down so that they are horizontal to the ground, and then they will produce a better crop of fruit, and are very easily gathered. This can also be done with apples and pears.

Cherries are fairly tolerant as to soil, as long as it is well-drained, preferring it slightly on the acid side. They crop best under conditions of moderately light rainfall. The best time to plant is October and November.

Propagation is by seed when growing wild, and by grafting if cultivated.

Plums, Greengages and Damsons   The parents of the cultivated plum, with all the varieties we now have, are the Sloe or Blackthorn, *P. spinosa*, and the Cherry Plum or Myrobalan, *P. cerasifera*. The sloe is the wild plum of Western Europe and Zone 4 and makes a very small tree with spiny branches, less than 10 ft (3 m) with ½ in (1.2 cm) blue-black fruit with a green, sharp-flavoured flesh. They are only used for making wine and sloe gin. The cherry plum is a native of Western Asia, the Caucasus and the Balkans and Zone 3 but grows wild in Britain, producing a mass of small white flowers in March; but the fruit is not prolific and is rather small, less than 1 in (2.5 cm) and tasteless, first green, then red or yellow. The Bullace, *P. insititia*, has larger fruits than the sloe and grows to a greater-sized tree, though only seen in the wild now, and seldom planted.

The large cultivated plum is now called *P. domestica*, with greenish-white flowers and glossy oval leaves. There are various good cooking varieties, of which I like 'Early Rivers', fruiting late July and early August and partly self-fertile; and 'Czar', fruiting early August and self-fertile. Both these have small round black fruit, but bear heavy crops; two more slightly pear-shaped and larger plums are both self-fertile, and fruiting mid to late August, 'Pershore Egg' being greenish-yellow and 'Purple Pershore' a dark red. The last two are not quite so flavoursome for cooking in pies and stewing, but make excellent jam.

The most famous dessert and cooking plum is the 'Victoria', with large pinkish-red fruit ripening in late August. It is very hardy, self-fertile and will grow under orchard conditions in Britain. It was discovered in a Sussex wood about 1840. For superb flavour for eating raw the plum 'Kirke's Blue' has a lovely round purple-red fruit with an attractive bluish bloom, but it is, like all good things, a poor cropper, doing so in early September, and unfortunately is self-incompatible. 'Coe's Golden Drop' has similar drawbacks but is a delicious-flavoured golden-yellow plum. These two both do very much better on a sunny warm wall. If there is only room for one plum tree in the garden choose 'Victoria', for its mid-season flowering makes it a good pollinator for any tree you might add to your stock later, as it will cover other early or late blossoming varieties.

But my favourite of the plum family are the greengages and yellowgages, *P. domestica italica*. They are smaller and round, ripening bright yellow or remaining a soft green, but delicious to eat raw with a lovely scent and flavour. The self-fertile kinds with white flowers are 'Ouillins Golden Gage' fruiting mid-August. It is found growing wild in Asia Minor, a small sturdy tree, which was re-introduced to England from France about 1725 where it is known as the 'Reine Claude'. Another of these old varieties is 'Early Transparent' with

19 *Wisteria sinensis*: Chinese Wisteria, with Clematis 'Niobe'

20 *Pyrus communis* 'Conference': Pear

golden fruit with a light bloom and red mottling. This fruits in mid- to late August, followed by the larger American yellowish-green variety 'Denniston's Superb', both self-fertile.

There are several plums that are gage-like in flavour and plum-like in size and colouring. The best of these is 'Golden Transparent', a large round golden-yellow fruit, dotted with red and ripening in October. It is self-fertile, but does need a warm wall in a sheltered garden, as it is not completely hardy.

Lastly, there are the Damsons, *P. domestica damascena*, with their rich sweet flavour. They are blue-black with little bloom, small and oval. They are quite delicious cooked or made into jam. They are all self-fertile, with white flowers; 'Merryweather' fruits in early September and 'Farleigh Damson' in mid-September. The 'Merryweather' has a larger fruit which is preferable, as the multitude of stones produced when cooking the ordinary damsons is perhaps the reason for their decline in popularity of late. For damsons are easily grown in the garden and make elegant standard trees.

Plums grow well on any reasonable well-drained soil, but they are not happy on extreme forms of clay, sand or chalk, and need shelter from east winds.

Plums are usually budded on to rootstocks of 'St. Julien A', but this produces quite a large tree for the garden. However, on the dwarfing rootstock 'Pixy' the growth is about half the size and ideal where space is restricted. These rootstocks can also be used for damsons, but they produce smaller trees.

CHAPTER 3

Special Ways to Grow Trees

Full-size trees are lovely to have on a property and even in a small area one or two specimens placed strategically — on a lawn or by a pool — can give the perfect touch to the design of the garden.

When you are choosing your tree think of the shape it grows — spreading, pyramidal or weeping — and fill in the surrounding ground with smaller trees or shrubs of a complementary shape and also plant ground cover to show up the foliage and flowers of the plantings above it. But you can change the pattern of your garden around, like shifting a kaleidoscope, by growing in large tubs.

Many trees will do well in a big container, especially the ones like the fig which likes a restricted root-run. They can be placed on a terrace, gracing a flight of steps, or near the house so that they are more easily seen and yet can be moved as they grow, back further into the garden proper, to be viewed from a distance. Another fruit, the apricot 'Moorpark', will also do well in a container, and so will a sweet cherry, which produces a good crop of fruit, with the roots checked.

Bay trees are often grown in tubs, and sometimes shaped as a topiary; they should be pruned and clipped in July. Eucalyptus is also effective, and choose the variety *E. gunnii* which is the hardiest, as the roots of container plants are more susceptible to frost and should be protected by wrapping the pot or tub with sacking to mollify any intense cold. This variety has two kinds of leaves, the young being glaucous circular discs and the older becoming long, narrow and pointed. Late in the season it produces yellow-stamened white flowers.

The paulownia, which produces great 1 ft (30 cm) long leaves if pruned to the ground each spring, also makes an interesting talking point when grown in a tub; though with this harsh treatment it will produce none of its fascinating fox-glove-like mauve flowers. There is a miniature privet, *Ligustrum sinense nanum*, which has dense spikes of creamy-white flowers, and is ideal for pot growing as it tolerates dry soils. Rhododendrons, which would become too sprawling and vast for an average garden, can be grown very successfully in tubs, especially if you have clay soil, which I have, and which they hate. I planted two very choice winter-flowering rhododendrons in ericaceous soil and my little trees have produced a mass of flower each year and can be judiciously pruned to a nice round shape; for maximum flowers always remove all the old flowerheads. The Cabbage Tree or Palm Lily, *Cordyline australis*, is a very attractive palm to grow in a tub and gives an exotic air to the surrounding scene, and it is better for a container than the Chusan Palm (see Chapter 1).

Weeping trees are also very effective grown in this way and evergreens look particularly good in a tub, but care must be taken to make sure they never dry out, by regular watering and mulching, especially in long dry periods. Another advantage of a tub is that you can grow-on a young, perhaps tender specimen, nurturing it till it is well established and till you have found the perfect place for it in the garden; and of course, if you ever move house, you can take your tub trees with you!

Another way to vary your trees is to grow the dwarf varieties, either in weeping or standard form. Cotoneaster is very showy, and I have seen a very attractive half-standard holly barely 3 ft (1 m) high and covered with berries, either planted in the border, or this can be tub-grown as well. This variety is a new American holly, *Ilex* 'Blue Girl', with shiny blue-green leaves contrasting beautifully with the fat glossy red fruits.

When a tree is tender and subject to damage from cold winds, it is an excellent idea to plant it against a sheltered wall. Here, it can either be allowed to grow up and top the wall, or it can be espaliered or grown in fan or cordon shape. It will flower and fruit so much better with this added protection and is so easy to cover from frost, or bird damage to fruit, by dropping a sheet of polythene over the branches from the top of the wall, when necessary.

Trees can also be grown as a tough barrier or wind-break, to divide up a garden or give shelter and privacy to a particular area of it. Hornbeam or beech make a very good hedge, *Carpinus betulus* being the best of the hornbeams for hedging and *Fagus sylvatica* the most suitable beech (see Chapter 1). The Holm Oak, *Quercus ilex*, can be clipped to shape and makes an evergreen hedge so that there is protection and privacy all the year. The privet, *Ligustrum*, is a familiar hedge and needs clipping in spring and again in late summer, otherwise it grows far too fast and blocks out the light, and sometimes the view. Another tree that gives a quick-growing screen is *Acer negundo*. The red-twigged form of the lime, *Tilia platyphyllos* 'Rubra', can be grown as a very successful hedge or pleached, the bright reddish-brown branches looking very cheerful during winter. It tolerates hard pruning and has a neat upright form of growth. Two other trees worth thinking about as colourful hedges are *Viburnum tinus* and *Tamarix*.

Bear in mind, should you be lucky enough to have a garden surrounded by high brick walls, that you have to allow for the wind getting within its confines and then it eddies and swirls around and can cause damage, so a shelter of trees planted strategically across the garden can help to mitigate this tendency.

Trees make good hosts for plants like clematis and when a plant is chosen that flowers at a different time, you will have two flowerings a year in the same space. I grow a white clematis up a holly and a pink one up a prunus, which I feel is using the available space in the garden to good effect. I have just planted an 'Alberic Barbier' rose at the base of my apple tree; 'Wedding Day' is another rose that does particularly well, but there are several others of different shades of flower, which will climb up without harming their host and produce stunningly effective combinations with tall old trees.

Pleaching gives a very graceful appearance to the garden. Trees are planted about 6 ft (2 m) apart and their branches intertwined as they grow so that they form a hedge. A double row makes a lovely walk and there is a famous planting of hornbeam at Hidcote Manor in Gloucestershire, where the pleached trees are as on stilts, trimmed and squared off so that their trunks are bare to 4 ft (1.2 m) above the ground. There is a pretty pleached lime tree walk which encloses the Sunken Garden in Kensington Gardens in London. Pleaching is also used to form a tunnel with the branches meeting overhead. There is a magnificent laburnum one at Bodnant Gardens in North Wales. But for the more modest garden, an arch, either the traditional curved shape or a crown arch, is very decorative and one of the many structures that can be obtained which are excellent for smothering with quick-growing, flowering, and if possible, scented blooms.

The pergola, like the tunnel, has a walk enclosed by two walls of plants, but is usually open at the top. A smaller pergola can also be made by placing two arches in the form of a cross, inside which you can have some form of seating or sculpture. Scent is very important for an arbour, which can be placed in a corner of the garden with a seat inside, so that you glimpse the setting from a different angle and enjoy the sights and fragrances of your garden scheme. There is also a structure of French origin called a bagatelle which has an upright circular 7 ft (2 m) high frame, inside which you plant your tree, a weeping form being particularly effective as it grows up and cascades over the sides of the frame, which can also accommodate a clematis or rose. This bagatelle looks good on grass or in an orchard, as long as the surrounding shade is not too dense.

Lastly, small trees planted in a sunken area give the very best of their foliage and flowers with the protection from the wind, and they are more easily admired from above or nearby.

As I have mentioned elsewhere, always try to go to a local nursery, where they grow their own plants and trees rather than to a Garden Centre where they often buy in, perhaps from afar, and do not necessarily know so much about the planting, positioning, and suitability of soil and temperature for the tree you have in mind for your size of garden. Many nurserymen will visit your garden and advise you on the best trees to use, and it is worth having the benefit of their expertise.

The right choice of trees will enhance and grace your garden for many years to come, and will grow to maturity, perhaps for others to enjoy in the future. To plant and nurture a plot of land is, I think, one of the most satisfying pleasures there are.

CHECKLIST

For particular varieties, see under the individual tree description in Chapter One

Trees with Scented Flowers
Acacia
Aesculus
Cedrela
Crataegus
Drimys
Elaeagnus
Eucalyptus
Eucryphia
Euodia
Gleditsia
Hamamelis
Idesia
Itea
Ligustrum
Liquidambar
Magnolia
Malus
Myrtus
Oxydendrum
Paulownia
Ptelea
Robinia
Stewartia
Styrax
Syringa
Tilia
Wisteria
Zelkova

Trees with Attractive Bark or Twigs
Acer
Arbutus
Betula
Eucalyptus
Fraxinus
Parrotia
Platanus
Prunus
Salix

Sorbus
Stewartia
Tilia
Zelkova

Weeping Trees
Alnus
Betula
Cotoneaster
Crataegus
Fagus
Fraxinus
Ilex
Malus
Morus
Populus
Prunus
Pyrus
Salix
Sophora
Tilia
Ulmus

Winter-Flowering Trees
Acacia
Arbutus
Ceanothus
Cornus
Corylus
Eucryphia
Hamamelis
Magnolia
Myrtus
Parrotia
Prunus
Rhododendron
Viburnum

Trees with Autumn Leaf Colour
Acer
Amelanchier
Betula

Carpinus
Cercidiphyllum
Crataegus
Fagus
Fraxinus
Ginkgo
Liquidambar
Malus
Morus
Nyssa
Ostrya
Parrotia
Populus
Prunus
Quercus
Rhus
Sassafras
Sorbus
Stewartia
Tilia
Ulmus
Zelkova

Trees that Grow in Erect Form
Acer
Betula
Carpinus
Crataegus
Eucryphia
Fagus
Ilex
Koelreuteria
Liriodendron
Malus
Populus
Prunus
Quercus
Salix
Sorbus
Ulmus
Zelkova

Trees with Silver or Grey Leaves

Acer
Crataegus
Elaeagnus
Eucalyptus
Fraxinus
Populus
Pyrus
Salix
Sorbus
Tilia

Trees with Ornamental Fruit

Ailanthus
Alnus
Arbutus
Castanea
Catalpa
Cercis
Cornus
Cotoneaster
Crataegus
Fraxinus
Gleditsia
Idesia
Ilex
Koelreuteria
Malus
Ostrya
Prunus
Pterocarya
Rhus
Sorbus

Trees for Seaside Gardens

Arbutus
Castanea
Crataegus
Eucalyptus
Fraxinus
Laurus
Populus
Quercus
Salix
Sorbus

Trees for Tiny Gardens

Acer
Alnus
Amelanchier
Aralia
Betula
Carpinus
Cercis
Cornus
Cotoneaster
Crataegus
Cydonia
Embothrium
Eucalyptus
Eucryphia
Fagus
Halesia
Hoheria
Ilex
Koelreuteria
Laburnum
Laurus
Malus
Mespilus
Morus
Populus
Prunus
Pyrus
Quercus
Rhus
Robinia
Salix
Sophora
Sorbus
Stewartia
Styrax
Syringa
Tamarix
Tilia

Trees for Industrial Atmospheres

Acer
Aesculus
Ailanthus
Alnus
Amelanchier

Betula
Carpinus
Catalpa
Crataegus
Davidia
Eucalyptus
Fraxinus
Ilex
Laburnum
Ligustrum
Liriodendron
Malus
Platanus
Populus
Prunus
Pterocarya
Pyrus
Quercus
Rhus
Robinia
Salix
Sorbus
Tilia

Trees for Large Gardens

Acer
Fraxinus
Ginkgo
Gleditsia
Platanus
Robinia
Quercus

Trees for Clay Soils

Acer
Aesculus
Alnus
Betula
Carpinus
Crataegus
Eucalyptus
Fraxinus
Ilex
Laburnum
Malus
Populus

Prunus
Quercus
Salix
Sorbus
Tilia
Ulmus

Trees for Acid Soils
Embothrium
Halesia
Liquidambar
Magnolia
Nothofagus
Nyssa
Oxydendrum
Quercus
Rhododendron
Stewartia
Styrax

Trees for Dry Sites
Castanea
Populus

Robinia
Ulmus

Trees for Damp Sites
Alnus
Amelanchier
Betula
Crataegus
Liquidambar
Mespilus
Nyssa
Populus
Pterocarya
Pyrus
Salix
Sorbus

Trees for Shady Sites
Acer
Fagus
Ilex
Prunus
Quercus

Trees for Tubs
Cordyline
Eucalyptus
Ilex
Laurus
Ligustrum
Paulownia

Trees for Screening and for Exposed Sites
Acer
Betula
Crataegus
Eucalyptus
Fagus
Fraxinus
Laburnum
Populus
Quercus
Salix
Sorbus
Tilia
Ulmus

CHAPTER 4

Detailed Reference Table of Trees Described

Key
1 Name of tree
2 Place of origin
3 Evergreen or Deciduous
4 Maximum height of tree
5 Colour of flower
6 Scent: 1 = strong, 2 = good, 3 = faint, 4 = none
7 Flowering time (months 1–12)
8 Soil: A = acid, B = neutral, C = alkaline, D = well-drained
9 Position: S = sun, Sh = shade, T = tender, needing shelter
10 Pruning: x = hard, y = shaping and removal of dead wood, z = very little or none
11 Propagation: Sd = seed, Ctg = cuttings, Lyg = layering, Gr = grafting, Srs = suckers, var = varieties (months 1–12)
12 Hardiness: Zone 5 = $-20°$ to $-10°$F, Zone 6 = $-10°$ to $0°$F, Zone 7 = $0°$ to $10°$F, Zone 8 = $10°$ to $20°$F, Zone 9 = $20°$ to $30°$F, Zone 10 = $30°$ to $40°$F

1	2	3	4	5
Acacia	Australia	E	10–20 ft (3–6 m)	yellow
Acer	Europe, Far East & North America	D	1–100 ft (0.3–30 m)	white to purple
Aesculus	Numerous	D	4–100 ft (1.2–30 m)	white to dark red
Ailanthus	China	D	to 70 ft (to 20 m)	yellowish/green
Albizia	Western Asia	D	to 40 ft (to 12 m)	pink
Alnus	Europe, Asia & North America	D	30–80 ft (10–25 m)	yellowish/green
Amelanchier	Europe & North America	D	30–50 ft (10–15 m)	white
Aralia	Asia & America	D	to 45 ft (to 14 m)	white/greenish white
Arbutus	Mediterranean & Eire	E	15–30ft (5–10 m)	pinky/white
Betula	Numerous, incl. Greenland	D	to 50 ft (to 15 m)	yellowish/green
Buddleia	China, Chile & Himalayas	D	8–15 ft (2.5–5 m)	white, orange, pink-purple
Carpinus	Europe, Japan & North America	D	30–75 ft (10–23 m)	pink or green
Castanea	Europe, North Africa, China, Japan, USA	D	30–100 ft (10–30 m)	cream
Catalpa	Asia & North America	D	15–65 ft (5–19 m)	white spotted purple & yellow
Ceanothus arboreus	California, var. Cornwall	E	to 40 ft (to 12 m)	deep blue
Cedrela sinensis	North & West China	D	to 70 ft (to 20 m)	white
Cercidiphyllum	Japan & China	D	50–100 ft (15–30 m)	red
Cercis	East Mediterranean & North America	D	to 30 ft (to 10 m)	rosy-lilac
Chionanthus	China & North America	D	20–30 ft (6–10 m)	white
Cornus	Europe, China, Japan, North America, India	D & E	10–60 ft (3–18 m)	yellow, white, greenish
Corylus	Europe, West Asia, North Africa, California	D	10–80 ft (3–25 m)	yellow & crimson
Cotoneaster	Himalaya	D & E	15–40 ft (5–12 m)	white tinged pink
Crataegus	Asia & Asia Minor, North America, North Africa, Europe	D	20–30 ft (6–10 m)	white & red
Cydonia	Southern Europe, Iran	D	to 25 ft (to 8 m)	white & pink

6	7	8	9	10	11	12
1	1–11	B	S/T	y	Sd 4 or Ctg 9	6–10
2	4–5	B	S	y	Sd; var Gr	2–5
2–3	5/7–8	B	S	z	Sd & Srs	3–7
3	7	Any	S/½Sh	y	Sd or Srs	4
4	6–7	B	S/T	z	Sd 4 or 9	7
4	2–4	B moist	S or Sh	z	Sd or srs; var Gr	2–5
4	5	B/D	S/½Sh	y	Sd 2 or Ctg 7	4
4	8	B	S/½Sh	y4	Sd 4 or Srs	3 & 4
4	10–12	B/C	S/T	z	Sd 2	6
4	3–5	Any	S or Sh	y	Sd	2–7
1	5–10	B	S	x or y	Ctg 9	5
4	4/5	C	S/½Sh	z	Sd or Srs; var Gr	2–5
4	6/7	B dry	S/Sh	z	Sd	4–5
4	7/8	B/D	S	y	Sd or Ctg	4
3	4 onwards	B/D	S/T	y 4	Air Ctg	6–7
1	6	B	S/½Sh	y	Sd or Srs	5
1	4	AB	S/½Sh	z	Sd 2 or Lyg 7	4
4	5	B/D	S	z	Sd or Srs	4 & 6
4 & 3	6/7 & 5/6	B	S	y	Gr & Sd	5 & 4
4	2 & 5/6	B/A	S/½Sh	y	Sd, Lyg, Ctg	4–8
4	2/3	B	S	y	Sd, Lyg, Srs	3–5
4	5/6	B/D	S/½Sh	y	Ctg 6–8	7
1	5 & 6	B	S or Sh	y	Sd; var Gr	4 & 5
4	5	B	S	y	Ctg 7	4

1	2	3	4	5
Davidia	Central & West China	D	20–65 ft (6–19 m)	white tinged green
Diospyros	Far East & North America	D & E	30–65 ft (10–19 m)	pale yellow
Drimys	South & Central America	E	8–25 ft (2.5–8 m)	ivory-white
Elaeagnus	Japan, temperate areas of Asia & Europe	D & E	15–20 ft (5–6 m)	pale yellow
Embothrium	Chile	E	20–40 ft (6–12 m)	scarlet
Eucalyptus	Australia	E	20–100 ft (6–30 m)	white, red or yellow
Eucryphia	Chile & Tasmania	E	12–15 ft (4–5 m)	white
Euodia	China & Korea	D & E	to 50 ft (to 15 m)	white
Fagus	Europe, North America & Asia	D	35–120 ft (11–35 m)	creamy
Ficus carica	West Asia & Eastern Mediterranean	D	to 30 ft (to 10 m)	greenish/white
Fraxinus	Europe, South-west USA & Asia Minor	D	20–130 ft (6–40 m)	creamy/white or green/yellow
Ginkgo biloba	East China	D	to 100 ft (to 30 m)	greenish/yellow/orange
Gleditsia	Japan, North Iran, Canada & Central & Eastern USA	D	35–140 ft (11–43 m)	yellowy/green
Halesia	South Eastern USA	D	35–90 ft (11–28 m)	pure white
Hamamelis	China, Japan & USA	D	6–25 ft (2–8 m)	yellows
Hoheria	New Zealand	D/E	10–45 ft (3–14 m)	white
Idesia	Japan, China	D	to 45 ft (to 14 m)	pale green
Ilex	Western & Southern Europe, West Asia to China, North Africa, Northern USA	D & E	10–60 ft (3–18 m)	white
Itea	China, Eastern USA	D & E	5–8 ft (1.2–2.5 m)	yellow-green
Juglans	Eastern North America, Japan, China, South Eastern Canada	D	50–150 ft (15–45 m)	greenish
Koelreuteria	China & Japan	D	30–50 ft (10–15 m)	yellow
Laburnum	Central & Southern Europe	D	13–20 ft (4–6 m)	yellow

6	7	8	9	10	11	12
4	5	B	S/½Sh	y	Sd 4 or Ctg 7	5 & 6
4	7	B/D	S	z	Sd or Gr	4 & 7
1	5/6	B	S/T	y	Ctg 6/7 or Lyg 6	6/7
1	5/6	B dry	S	y	Sd 2	2
4	5/6	A moist	Sh/T	z	Ctg 4	7/8
1	7/8	B	S/T	x5 or y	Sd 4; var. Gr	6/7/10
2	8–12	A/B	S/½Sh	z	Sd 2/3	6/7
1	8–9	B	S	y	Sd	5
4	5	B/D	S/Sh	z	Sd, Gr, Srs	3 & 4
4	5	B poor	S	y	Srs, Ctg	6
4 & 2	4 & 5	B	S/½Sh	y	Sd; var Gar	3 & 5
3	3	B or C	S/½Sh	z	Sd or Gr	4
1	6	B/D	S/½Sh	y	Sd 4	4–6
4	4/5	A	S	y	Sd 9, Lyg, Ctg	4–5
1	10–11 & 12–3	AB/D	S/½Sh	z	Gr or Lyg	4 & 5
3	7–8	B	S/T	z	Lyg or Ctg	6/7
1	6/7	AB/D	S	z	Sd or Gr	5 & 6
2	5/6	B & A	S/½Sh	y	Ctg 8 or Sd	5–8
1	7/8 or 7/9	BA	S/½Sh	z	Ctg 9	6–7
4	6/7	B/D	S/T	y 8	Gr	3–6
4	7/8	B dry	S	z	Sd 2 or Ctg	5
4	5/6	BC	S or Sh	x	Sd 2 or Gr 4	4/5

1	2	3	4	5
Lagerstroemia indica	China, Korea	D	to 30 ft (to 10 m)	lilac-pink
Laurus	Mediterranean region	E	to 60 ft (to 18 m)	yellowish/green
Ligustrum	China	D & E	30–50 ft (10–15 m)	white
Liquidambar	Eastern USA, Taiwan & Southern China, Asia Minor	D	20–140 ft (6–43 m)	greenish/yellow
Liriodendron	China, Eastern North America	D	50–160 ft (15–50 m)	greenish/yellow
Magnolia	Himalayas, China, Japan, South Eastern USA	D & E	var. 6–100 ft (var 2–30 m)	white, rose, cream, purple
Malus	Europe & Asia	D	10–50 ft (3–15 m)	white, rose/pink
Mespilus germanica	Asia Minor, South Eastern Europe	D	to 20 ft (to 6 m)	white
Morus	Asia & West Asia	D	20–30 ft (6–10 m)	greenish
Myrtus	Mediterranean, Chile	E	8–25 ft (2.5–8 m)	creamy
Nothofagus	New Zealand, Australia, Chile	D & E	3–110 ft (1–33 m)	yellowy/green
Nyssa	Central & Southern Mexico, Southern Canada, Eastern USA	D	20–100 ft (6–30 m)	yellowy/green
Ostrya	Southern Europe, Japan, Eastern North America	D	to 65 ft (to 19 m)	green/yellow & red
Oxydendrum	Eastern USA	D	20–75 ft (6–23 m)	white
Parrotia	North Iran & Caucasus	D	to 50 ft (to 15 m)	crimson stamens
Paulownia	China	D	to 30/40 ft (to 10/12 m)	heliotrope
Picrasma	Japan, China, Korea, India	D	to 40 ft (to 12 m)	greenish/yellow
Platanus	Eastern USA, South Ontario, Southern Europe	D	to 150 ft (to 45 m)	yellow & reddish
Populus	West, Central & Southern Europe, China, Western Asia, Ontario, N. USA	D	65–130 ft (19–40 m)	yellow, green & red
Prunus	China, Japan, Asia, Europe, North USA	D & E	8–100 ft (2.5–30 m)	white, cream, pink, red
Ptelea	Eastern North America, Mexico	D	10–20 ft (3–6 m)	yellowish/white
Pterocarya	Caucasus, North Iran, China	D	40–100 ft (12–30 m)	green

6	7	8	9	10	11	12
4	7	B	S/T	y 1 & y 8	Sd or Ctg	7
4	4	B/D	S	x	Sd, Ctg, Lyg, Srs	5/6
1	7 or 8–9	B	S/½Sh	y	Ctg 8 or 9	6/7
4	5	A/D	S/½Sh	y 1	Lyg 4	5–7
1	5–7	B deep	S	z	Sd; var Gr	4 & 7
1	var 2–9	A/B	S/½Sh	z & y 4	Lyg 5 or Ctg 6	5–9
1 or 3	4–6	B	S	y	Sd, Lyg or Gr	2–5
3	5/7	B/D	S/T	y 11	Sd 10	5
4	4	B/D	S	x/y	Ctg 9/10, Lyg 10	4 & 6
1	7 & 8–9	B/D	S/T	z	Ctg 8	6 & 8
4	4–5	B/D	S/½Sh	z	Ctg or Lyg	7
4	6	A moist	S/½Sh	z	Sd 8	4
4	4	B	S/½Sh	z	Sd, Ctg, Lyg, Gr	5
1	7/8	AB moist	S/Sh	y	Sd 2, Lyg, Ctg	5
4	3	BC/D	S/½Sh	z, x on wall	Sd Lyg 9	5
1	5	B/D	S/T	x or z	Sd or Ctg	5 & 7
3	6	AB or C/D	S/½Sh	y	Sd, Ctg, Srs or Gr	4
4	5	B/D	S	x or z	Sd, Lyg, or Ctg	4, 5, 6
4	2–5	B moist	S	y 8	Ctg	2–5
3	1–6	BC	S/½T	y	Sd or Gr	3–6
1	6/7	B	½Sh	x or y	Sd or Ctg	4
4	4	B moist	S	y	Sd or Gr	5 & 6

1	2	3	4	5
Pyrus	Caucasus, Southern Europe	D	to 50 ft (to 15 m)	creamy, pure-white
Quercus	Eastern USA, South-Eastern Canada, Southern Europe, Asia Minor, North Africa	D & E	25–160 ft (8–50 m)	green or yellow
Rhododendron arboreum	Himalaya	E	30–50 ft (10–15 m)	white, red or rose
Rhus	China, Korea, Japan, Eastern North America	D & E	25–65 ft (8–19 m)	greeny/white
Robinia	North Mexico, USA	D	12–80 ft (4–25 m)	white, pink
Salix	Europe, Asia, China, Himalaya, North Africa	D	3 in (8 cm) or 12–80 ft (4–25 m)	yellow, green, silver-grey
Sassafras	Eastern USA	D	20–100 ft (6–30 m)	yellowy/green
Sophora	South Western USA, Chile, New Zealand, China	D & E	to 40 ft (to 12 m)	yellow or pink or creamy
Sorbus	China, Japan, Kashmir, Europe, Asia, North Africa	D	to 65 ft (to 19 m)	white or pink
Stewartia	China, Japan, Korea, North USA	D	8–15+ ft (2.5–5+ m)	white
Styrax	Japan, China, South-Eastern USA	D	6–35 ft (2–11 m)	white
Syringa	Eastern Europe, China, Japan	D	6–20 ft (2–6 m)	white, yellow red to purple
Tamarix	South Western & Eastern Europe, West & Central Asia	D & E	3–12 ft (1–4 m)	white, shades of pink
Tilia	Europe, China, Central & Eastern North USA, South-Eastern Canada	D	30–130 ft (10–40 m)	creamy/white, yellow
Trachycarpus	Central China	E	10–40 ft (3–12 m)	yellow
Ulmus	British Isles, Europe, North & West Asia, China, Japan	D	20–150 ft (6–45 m)	reddish or pale green
Viburnum	Mediterranean, China, Korea & Himalayas	D & E	5–15 ft (1.5–5 m)	white & creamy-white
Wisteria	China, Japan & USA	D	4–10 ft (1.2–3 m)	white, pink, lilac, purple
Zelkova	Japan, Korea, China, Caucasus, Crete	D	30–80 ft (10–25 m)	green or white

6	7	8	9	10	11	12
3	4	B	S	y	Gr or Sd	4 & 5
4	3–6	A, B or C	S/½Sh	z	Sd	4–8
4	1–5	A moist	S/½Sh	z	Lyg 7 or 8	6
4	6/7	B poor	S/½Sh	x or y 2	Ctg 3, Lyg 3	5
1 & 3	5/6	B dry	S	y	Sd or Srs, Gr	3
4	3/4	AB or B	S	x or y	Ctg 11–2 or Setts	2–6
4	5	A/D	Woodland	y	Sd or Root Srs	4
4	5/6 & 9	B rich	S/T	y	Sd	7–9
4	5/6	B/D	S	y	Sd 2 or Gr	2–5
4 & 1	6–8	A moist	½Sh/T	y	Ctg 7 or 8	5
4 & 1	6–7	A moist	S/½Sh	z	Sd 2 or Ctg 7–8	5
1	5–6	BC	S	x or y	Gr, Lyg, Ctg	4–5
2 & 4	5 & 8–10	AB/D	S	y2 & 8	Ctg 10	4–5
1	6/7	B	S/Sh	y 1 or 2	Gr, Lyg or Srs	2–5
2	5/6	B/D	S/T	z	Sd or Srs	6/7
4	2–4 or 8–9	B	S	y	Lyg or Srs	2–5
2 & 4	11–7	B	S/½Sh	y or x	Ctg 7	3
1 & 2	5/6	B	S	x	Ctg 8	5
1	4 & 5	B/D	S/½Sh	y	Sd or Gr	5 & 6

APPENDIX I

List of Nurseries

GREAT BRITAIN

The Garden Centre at Alexandra
  Palace,
London N22 4BB
Tel: 01–444–2555

C.H. Ashby & Son,
Nursery and Garden Centre,
Woodcote,
Oxfordshire
Tel: 0491–680335

Bodnant Garden Nursery,
Tal-y-Cafn,
Colwyn Bay,
Clwyd,
Wales LL28 5RE
Tel: 0492–650–460

Bressingham Gardens,
Diss,
Norfolk IP22 2AB
(*B. alba* 'Golden Cloud' only)
Tel: 037–988–464

Filsham Nurseries,
Charles Road West,
St Leonards-on-Sea,
East Sussex
Tel: 0424–421663

Glyndley Garden Centre,
Hailsham Road,
Stone Cross,
Sussex
Tel: 0323–763240

Hilliers Nurseries (Winchester) Ltd,
Ampfield House,
Ampfield,
Nr. Romsey,
Hants
Tel: 0794–68733

Murrells Nursery,
Broomer's Hill Lane,
Pulborough,
West Sussex
Tel: 079–82–2771

140

Notcutts Nurseries Ltd,
Ipswich Road,
Woodbridge,
Suffolk
Tel: 03943–3600

R. & R. Saggers Plants,
High Street,
Newport,
Nr Saffron Walden,
Essex
Tel: 0799–40858

Clive Simms,
Woodhurst,
Essendine,
Stamford,
Lincs PE9 4LQ
Tel: 0780–55615

Toad Hall Garden Centre,
Marlow Road,
Henley-on-Thames,
Oxfordshire
Tel: 0491–574615

Whiteleggs Garden Centre,
Tonbridge Road,
Pembury,
Kent
Tel: 089–282–2636

The Plant Centre,
The Royal Horticultural Society
  Garden,
Wisley,
Woking,
Surrey GU23 6QB
Tel: 0483–224234

APPENDIX II
Conversion Tables

Fahrenheit — Celsius			Imperial	Metric
°F	°C		1 in	2.5 cm
−58	−50		6 in	15 cm
23	− 5		1 ft	30 cm
32	0		3 ft	91 cm
41	5		10 ft	3 m
50	10		20 ft	6 m
59	15		30 ft	9 m
68	20		60 ft	18 m

APPENDIX III
Glossary of Terms

Leaves and Flowers

Anther	The pollen-bearing part of the stamen.
Axil	The angle formed by a leaf or lateral branch with the stem, or of a vein with the midrib.
Bract	A modified, usually reduced leaf at the base of a flower-stalk, flower-cluster or shoot.
Circular	Completely round.
Compound	Composed of two or more similar parts.
Corymb	A flat-topped or dome-shaped flower head, with the outer flowers opening first.
Doubly serrate	Large teeth and small teeth alternating.
Elliptic	Widest at or about the middle, narrowing equally at both ends.
Filament	The stalk of a stamen.
Glabrous	Hairless.
Glaucous	Covered with a 'bloom', bluish-white or bluish-grey.
Incised	Sharply and usually deeply and irregularly cut.
Inflorescence	The flowering part of the plant or tree.
Lanceolate	Lance-shaped, widening above the base and long tapering to the apex.
Leaflet	Part of a compound leaf.
Lustrous	Shining.
Oblong	Longer than broad with nearly parallel sides.
Obovate	Inversely ovate.
Oval	Broadest at the middle.
Ovate	Broadest below the middle, like a hen's egg.
Palmate	Lobed or divided in hand-like fashion, usually five or seven lobed.
Panicle	Branching raceme.

Pedicel	The stalk of an individual flower in an inflorescence.
Peduncle	The stalk of a flower-cluster or a solitary flower.
Pinnate	With leaflets arranged on either side of a central stalk.
Pistil	The female organ of a flower comprising ovary, style and stigma.
Raceme	A simple elongated inflorescence with stalked flowers.
Samara	A fruit being a single wing.
Serrate	Saw-toothed (teeth pointing forward).
Sessile	Not stalked.
Spine	A sharp-pointed end of a branch or leaf.
Spur	A tubular projection from a flower; or a short stiff branchlet.
Stamen	The male organ of a flower comprising filament and anther.
Stigma	The summit of the pistil which receives the pollen; often sticky or feathery.
Style	The middle part of the pistil, often elongated between the ovary and stigma.
Umbel	A normally flat-topped inflorescence in which the pedicels or peduncles all arise from a common point.

Cultivation of Trees

Bush	With a stem of 2–3 ft (60–90 cm), the main branches arising close together to form the head.
Clone	Each of a group of individual trees derived from a single stem.
Columnar	Slim like a column.
Conical	Shaped like a cone.
Cordon	Single straight stem, usually grown at an oblique angle, which has short fruit spurs along its length.
Cultivar	Garden variety; or form found in the wild and maintained as a clone in cultivation.
Deciduous	A tree which loses all its leaves annually in the autumn.
Double leader	Where two competitive shoots are developing, one should be cut out to avoid acute-angle forking of the branches.
Dwarf pyramid	Shorter form of pyramid.
Espalier	A central vertical main stem, with pairs of horizontal branches growing out at right angles on each side.
Evergreen	A tree which retains its leaves throughout the year.
Fan	Trained flat against a wall or fence, with branches radiating from a short trunk like the ribs of a fan.
Fastigiate	The branches grow virtually parallel to each other in a close upwards direction.
Feathered	A young tree trained to form a standard or half-standard,

	while it still retains side branches on the main stem. The side branches are later removed.
Half-standard	With a trunk about 4 ft (1.2 m) from ground to first branch.
Head	The collection of branches on a standard or half-standard tree.
Hybrid	The result of a cross between two different species.
Lateral	On or at the side.
Leader	The single main leading shoot. In a mature tree, the length of trunk from ground level.
Maiden	A tree of one year's growth from a bud or graft.
Pendulous	Hanging or weeping
Pleaching	To intertwine the branches of trees to form a hedge.
Pollarding	A tree having the whole crown cut off, leaving it to send out new branches from the top of the stem.
Procumbent	Lying or creeping.
Prostrate	Lying flat on the ground.
Pyramid	A tree with a main stem from which, at around 1 ft (30 cm) from the ground, branches begin to radiate at intervals in gradually diminishing length.
Rootstock	The stock on which a scion is grafted, or a bud inserted.
Scion	A shoot used for grafting upon a rootstock.
Spindlebush	A cone-shaped tree with a single vertical stem. The side branches are tied down which induces the formation of buds.
Standard	With a trunk 5½ ft (1.5 m) from ground to first branch.
Suckering	Producing underground stems; or the shoots from the stock of a grafted tree.
Weeping	The branches are pendulous.
Whip-graft	To graft by fitting a tongue cut on the scion to a slit cut slopingly in the rootstock.

Hardiness Zone Maps

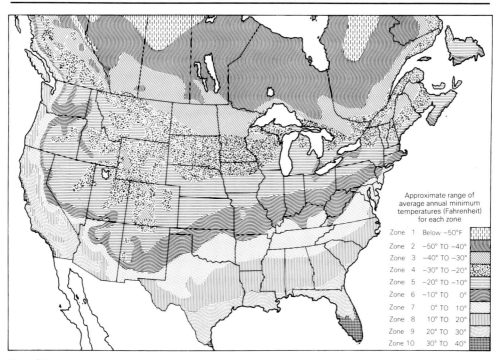

Approximate range of average annual minimum temperatures (Fahrenheit) for each zone		
Zone 1	Below −50°F	
Zone 2	−50° TO −40°	
Zone 3	−40° TO −30°	
Zone 4	−30° TO −20°	
Zone 5	−20° TO −10°	
Zone 6	−10° TO 0°	
Zone 7	0° TO 10°	
Zone 8	10° TO 20°	
Zone 9	20° TO 30°	
Zone 10	30° TO 40°	

Hardiness Zones of North America

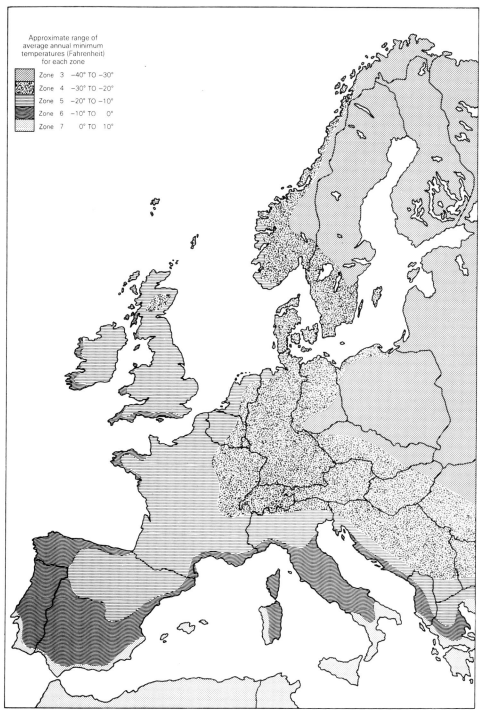

Approximate range of
average annual minimum
temperatures (Fahrenheit)
for each zone

Zone 3 −40° TO −30°
Zone 4 −30° TO −20°
Zone 5 −20° TO −10°
Zone 6 −10° TO   0°
Zone 7   0° TO 10°

Hardiness Zones of Europe

Bibliography

Bagenal, N.B., *The Fruit Grower's Handbook* (London and Melbourne, 1949)

Baker, Harry, *The Fruit Garden Displayed* (London, 1986)

Bean, W.J., *Ornamental Trees for Amateurs* (London, 1958)

Beckett, Kenneth A., *The Love of Trees* (London, 1975)

Crowther, D.S., *Fruit for Small Gardens* (London, 1949)

Dunkin, Henry, *The Pruning of Hardy Fruit Trees* (London, 1934)

Foster, Raymond, *The Garden in Autumn and Winter* (Newton Abbot, 1983)

Hay, Roy and Synge, Patrick M., *The Dictionary of Garden Plants* (London, 1975)

Hillier, *Manual of Trees and Shrubs* (Winchester, 1981)

Johns, C.A., *The Forest Trees of Britain* (London and New York, 1882)

Johns, Leslie, *Garden Trees* (Newton Abbot, 1973)

Johnson, Hugh, *The International Book of Trees* (London, 1973)

Kinahan, Sonia, *The Winter Flower Garden* (London and New York, 1985)

Lancaster, Roy, *Trees for Your Garden* (Nottingham, 1974)

Leathart, Scott, *Trees of the World* (London, New York, Sydney and Toronto, 1977)

The Macdonald Encyclopedia of Trees (London and Sydney, 1982)

Macoboy, Stirling, *Trees for Flower and Fragrance* (Sydney, Auckland, London and New York, 1986)

Mansfield, T.C., *Shrubs in Colour and Cultivation* (London, 1945)

Masefield, G.B., Wallis, M., Harrison, S.G. and Nicholson, B.E., *The Oxford Book of Food Plants* (Oxford, 1971)

Phillips, Roger, *Trees in Britain, Europe and North America* (London, 1978)

Polunin, Oleg, *Trees and Bushes of Britain and Europe* (Oxford, 1976)

Sweet, Arthur J., *Ornamental Shrubs and Trees, Their Selection and Pruning* (London, 1937)

Taylor, George M., *The Little Garden* (London, 1948)

Webster, A.D., *Hardy Ornamental Flowering Trees and Shrubs* (London, 1908)

Index